What's on the YOUR HOME OFFICE CD-ROM

The CD-ROM included with *YOUR HOME OFFICE* contains a variety of **software samples and shareware programs** designed to help you take advantage of the many resources available to you by computer **as you organize or upgrade your home office.** In addition, you get $15 worth of free time on CompuServe, the popular online service.

Here are the commercial demos you'll find on the CD:

- Personal Journal (interactive version of *The Wall Street Journal*)
- DiskNet (virus protection program)

In addition to these demos, you find these shareware programs:

- Frequent Flyer Manager
- PKZIP
- Understanding the Internet
- Business Letters
- Walnut Creek CDROM

You'll also discover the exciting world of CompuServe, where you can share information with people around the world. Included on this CD-ROM is WinCIM for Windows, a colorful, easy-to-use interface program, and $15 of online time through ZiffNet.

System Requirements

- 386DX-33 (486DX-33 or faster recommended)
- 4MB RAM (minimum)
- 4MB available on hard drive
- SuperVGA adapter (supporting 640 × 480 resolution and 256 colors) highly recommended
- Microsoft Mouse or 100 percent compatible
- Microsoft Windows 3.1 or higher
- MS-DOS 3.0 or higher
- Single-speed CD-ROM drive (double-speed recommended)

YOUR HOME OFFICE:
Total **Planning** on Your **Computer**

Patrice-Anne Rutledge

ZIFF-DAVIS PRESS
EMERYVILLE, CALIFORNIA

Editor	Margo Hill
Project Coordinator	Barbara Dahl
Proofreader	Vanessa Miller
Cover Design and Illustration	Regan Honda
Book Design	Regan Honda
Screen Graphics Editor	P. Diamond
Illustration	Sarah Ishida, Mina Reimer, and Cherie Plumlee
Word Processing	Howard Blechman
Page Layout	Alan Morgenegg, M. D. Barrera, and Tony Jonick
Indexer	Valerie Robbins

Ziff-Davis Press books are produced on a Macintosh computer system with the following applications: FrameMaker®, Microsoft® Word, QuarkXPress®, Adobe Illustrator®, Adobe Photoshop®, Adobe Streamline™, MacLink®*Plus*, Aldus® FreeHand™, Collage Plus™.

For information about U.S. rights and permissions, contact Chantal Tucker at Ziff-Davis Publishing, fax 212-503-5420.

If you have comments or questions or would like to receive a free catalog, call or write:
Ziff-Davis Press
5903 Christie Avenue
Emeryville, CA 94608
800-688-0448

ISBN 1-56276-327-X

Manufactured in the United States of America
10 9 8 7 6 5 4 3 2

To my mother, Phyllis L. Rutledge, and to the memory of my grand-mother, Violet Christina Sylvia, for their love, support, and encouragement.

Table of Contents

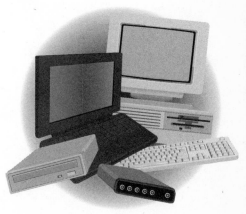

Special thanks go to Suzanne Anthony, Margaret Hill, and Barbara Dahl for their editorial expertise; Lysa Lewallen and Michael Delacy for their research assistance; and Stephen Delacy for his efforts in creating the accompanying CD-ROM.

This book is for anyone who wants to use the power of today's technology to work from a home-based or mobile office. Its goal is to show how anyone who's computer-literate—but not necessarily a computer expert—can use this technology to create a more flexible and rewarding way to work.

Your Home Office covers a lot of ground—everything from selecting basic hardware and software to connecting with remote networks to doing online research. Throughout the book I've tried to suggest the products that are the best in their field or offer the greatest value, as well as highlight some of the products that will be in the spotlight in the months to come. For more comprehensive coverage on computer equipment, see the *PC Magazine 1996 Computer Buyer's Guide*, also published by Ziff-Davis Press.

Most chapters that recommend specific products include a suggested retail price. This retail price should give you a way to compare product pricing on an equal basis, but probably won't be the price you'll actually pay when purchasing the product. By buying through the many discount avenues available, you can pay substantially less than the suggested retail price.

An added bonus comes with the book: a CD-ROM filled with demo, trial, and shareware programs suited to someone who works from home or a mobile office. We've included WinCIM, a program that provides a graphical interface for the CompuServe online service; Personal Journal software that includes a trial membership to this interactive version of *The Wall Street Journal*; a demo of Disk-Net virus protection software; and lots of shareware from Walnut Creek CDROM and ZiffNet. Some of the interesting shareware to check out: the WinHelp file Understanding the Internet, a collection of 600 sample business letters, the Time and Chaos Personal Information Manager, as well as the utility PkZip to help you "unzip" compressed files.

1

Is **Telecommuting** in Your **Future**?

According

to many business experts, telecommuting will be a commonplace work practice in the coming years. In many progressive organizations, the virtual office of the future is here today. Following the massive 1994 earthquake in Northridge, California, Pacific Bell implemented a major telecommuting program to get workers up and running despite road conditions that kept them from their offices. Even after the roads were clear again, many of the people affected by this earthquake continued to telecommute.

Natural disasters aren't the only reasons companies choose to implement telecommuting. The Clean Air Act of 1990, which requires certain companies with more than 100 employees to find ways to reduce worksite commuting, and the Family and Medical Leave Act of 1993, which provides up to 12 weeks unpaid leave per employee for family and medical situations, both encourage telecommuting and flexible work options. Companies are also moving toward telecommuting for many other reasons:

- To offer the flexible work schedules necessary to retain talented employees
- To allow parents to successfully combine a career and family obligations
- To reduce the exorbitant real estate costs of commercial space and increase profitability

Even in firms without official telecommuting programs, employees' requests to telecommute are receiving a positive response because today's technology makes telecommuting feasible and advantageous to both the employee and the company.

A recent survey conducted by industry analysts at the GartnerGroup offers some surprising insight into the growing popularity of telecommuting:

- More than 80 percent of all organizations will have at least 50 percent of their staff engage in some form of telecommuting by the year 1999.
- In 1993 the average number of telecommuters in the U.S. was 7.1 million people, up from 6.6 million in 1992.
- The average productivity increase per telecommuter, as measured by employers, ranged from 10 to 16 percent.
- The average telecommuter spends one day per week in the office.

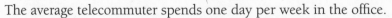

➡ The average annual facility cost savings per telecommuter is from $3,000 to $5,000, whereas the average investment per person is only $1,000 to $1,500.

Types of Telecommuting

Many jobs are ideally suited to telecommuting, either because they are computer- or telephone-intensive, or because they don't require the employee to be on-site the entire day. Careers suited to telecommuting include

➡ Sales representatives

➡ Technical support staffers

➡ Customer service representatives

➡ Writers

➡ Data entry workers

➡ Artists and designers

➡ Public relations professionals

➡ Computer programmers

➡ Editors

Other positions also offer the possibility of telecommuting, although many of these may only be part-time. Some examples would be managers, engineers, and consultants.

There are basically three kinds of telecommuting situations, and the type of technology you need depends on which situation you are in. These situations are

➡ Full-time home-based telecommuters. These telecommuters spend most of their work day in a home office with little or no need for field computing.

 Part-time telecommuters. These individuals spend part of their time in a traditional workplace and part working either at home or another location.

 Mobile telecommuters. These are the "road warriors" who spend most of their day in the field, traveling from location to location. Included here are sales representatives and field engineers.

People who spend time in more than one location, such as part-time or mobile telecommuters, may need to have both desktop and notebook computer systems or two desktop systems.

Criteria for Telecommuters

Although millions of people currently telecommute, working from home, particularly full-time, isn't for everyone. It takes a certain type of person working under certain circumstances to successfully work from home full-time on a long-term basis. According to the *Telecommuting Resource Guide* published by Pacific Bell, the ideal telecommuter is someone who

- Needs little supervision or feedback
- Requires limited social interaction
- Posseses excellent organizational and time management skills
- Is self-motivated
- Has demonstrated strong performance in the past
- Is a tenured employee who understands the company and its procedures
- Is a full-time, permanent employee

Advantages and Disadvantages of Telecommuting

In general, most people find working from home, either full- or part-time, to be a positive experience. But, as with every decision, telecommuting has both advantages and disadvantages. The following list applies primarily to those working from home full-time, but can also be considerations for those contemplating part-time telecommuting or working from a mobile office.

Advantages of Telecommuting

- You're in charge of your own space/environment.

➡ The time you spent commuting will be reduced or eliminated.

➡ You can be more productive and will face fewer interruptions.

➡ You have more control over your day.

➡ Working from home is often less stressful than working in a corporate office.

➡ You'll have more time to spend with your family.

Disadvantages of Telecommuting

➡ You may need to be careful to avoid feeling isolated.

➡ Being away from the office may mean you could be overlooked for promotional opportunities (the out-of-sight, out-of-mind mentality).

➡ You could be prone to home-based distractions (children, eating, TV) if you don't manage your time well.

Particularly if you're very gregarious and rely on the office for your social interactions, want to pursue the fast-track at your company, or don't manage your time well and tend to be disorganized, you will need to conquer these potential pitfalls to make telecommuting work for you. If any of these areas are a major concern to you, you might want to consider telecommuting only part-time. If you do plan to telecommute full-time, following are some suggestions.

How to Avoid Isolation

➡ Remain in frequent contact with office-based co-workers, either by phone or electronically via e-mail.

➡ Attend classes and seminars to keep current in your field and make contacts.

➡ If possible, visit your main office at least every week or two.

➡ Arrange your schedule so that you get out of the house at least several times a week during the work week.

How to Remain on the Fast Track

➡ Follow the tips for avoiding isolation to maintain close ties with your colleagues so they still feel you're part of the team.

Take the responsibility to publicize your accomplishments throughout your company since people may not be aware of your contributions now that you are working from home.

How to Manage Time and Avoid Distractions

 Make a schedule before you start telecommuting and stick to it.

➡ Create an invisible barrier between your workspace and your surroundings (children, pets, kitchen, TV, and so forth) and don't cross the barrier until it's time for you to take a break.

➡ Taking care of young children can be a full-time occupation itself, so plan a child-care strategy before you start telecommuting.

➡ Take a class on time management to learn how to effectively manage your time and yourself in your new environment.

For more information on the personal aspects of telecommuting, consult Appendix A.

➡ *Tips for Telecommuting Success*

Preston Gralla, executive editor for software libraries at Ziff-Davis Interactive, is a part-time telecommuter who successfully blends time spent working at both his corporate and home offices. "My job involves managing as well as writing," says Gralla. "It's hard to concentrate on writing and editing in the midst of office disruptions, so telecommuting is the perfect way to increase my productivity." Some of his suggestions for telecommuting success include the following:

➡ Make sure that your boss likes and supports the idea of telecommuting; make it a formal arrangement.

➡ Be sure that you still maintain a "presence" at work, even though you're not physically there (e-mail, phone, fax).

➡ Learn to deal with the jealousy and remarks of co-workers and be prepared to prove you are still contributing while working at home.

➡ *Tips for Telecommuting Success (Continued)*

➡ Be prepared to handle some of your own computer problems by educating yourself on your system and purchasing diagnostic software; develop a good rapport with your company's help desk.

➡ Invest in two phone lines: one for voice and one for fax/modem.

➡ If you don't want to purchase a fax machine, look into a fax receiving service, such as Delrina Fax MailBox, which receives faxes even if you're using your data line.

➡ Before you start telecommuting, determine what is best done at home and what needs to be done at the office.

2 Choosing Your New System

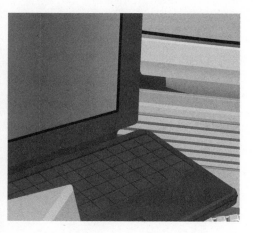

Your

company will probably provide the hardware you need for telecommuting. However, if you will be purchasing your own equipment or have a say in what equipment you receive, this chapter offers some valuable advice.

Rapidly changing technology makes purchasing a computer a difficult task. What is state of the art today can be on its way to obsolescence in a year. And falling prices on current technology make it challenging to determine how long to wait before buying. The "technobabble" presented in many computer ads and spoken by some computer salespersons can add further confusion. The best strategy is to determine what you need *now*, while planning for future expansion and upgradeability.

A nontechnical person really needs to understand only a few major technical concepts to select the right computer. When determining your hardware needs, the first thing you should do is decide whether you will need a desktop system, a notebook system, or both. This depends a lot on the kind of work that you do, how much time you spend at the computer, and where you will be working.

Purchasing a Desktop Computer

Most desktop computers are sold as complete systems, although there is usually a lot of flexibility in what each system contains. There are five main components to consider when purchasing a basic desktop computer system: processor, memory, monitor, hard drive, and floppy disk drive.

~💻~

Processor The main choice today for an IBM-compatible PC is between a 486-based processor and a Pentium. The processor runs your computer and determines how fast your computer will run. Your computer's speed is also indicated by its clock speed, measured in megahertz (MHz). This can vary anywhere from 25 to 100 MHz. A Pentium, essentially a 586-based processor, is the fastest system currently available. A 486 system has several options: SX, DX2, and DX4, each with increasing speed. An upgradable 486 DX processor with a speed of at least 66 MHz or a moderate speed (60 MHz) Pentium should be sufficient for most telecommuters' needs, unless you require super-fast processing for a particular reason.

In the Macintosh world, the Power Macintosh with its PowerPC 601 processor is a good choice for most business users. Depending on the model, speed on these systems ranges from 60 to 110 MHz. In addition, Power Macs can run DOS and Windows programs using SoftWindows software, developed by Insignia Systems. Also, by mid-1995, Apple won't be your only choice for purchasing a Macintosh-based computer. Power Computing, Radius, and Cutting Edge have all signed licensing agreements that will allow them to manufacture and sell Mac clones. Power Computing plans to market products that are equivalent to the Power Macintosh 7100 and 8100.

Memory Random access memory (RAM) is the memory that runs your software. RAM is referred to in terms of megabytes (MB). A basic computer system should have at least 8MB of RAM. If you are going to work with heavy graphics or database applications, you should invest in 16MB of RAM. Without sufficient RAM your computer will run slower, you won't be able to run as many programs simultaneously, and in some cases certain software won't function. Databases and CAD programs are particularly memory-intensive. Paradox 5, for example, requires 8MB of RAM, and Visual FoxPro requires 12MB. Before determining how much RAM you need, check the manuals for your major applications to check their memory requirements.

Monitors Most computer systems come with a standard-size color monitor along with a compatible video card. A Super VGA noninterlaced monitor offers the best resolution, less flickering, and the fastest screen refresh. If you will be doing extensive graphics work or for some reason need a larger monitor (17 inches or greater) you will pay up to $1,500 more than you would for a regular monitor. An antiglare and/or antiradiation screen is a good idea if you will be spending extended amounts of time in front of your monitor.

Hard Drive Your hard drive stores your programs and data. The latest in computer software is taking up more and more hard disk space, so this is one area in which you don't want to scrimp. The average system will probably have between

350 and 500MB (a hard drive's capacity is also measured in megabytes), although you may require more if you run a lot of specialized software or will be storing large databases or graphic files on your computer. Gigabyte (G) drives, equivalent to 1,000MB, are becoming popular with users who have high storage needs, and they are falling in price as well.

Floppy Disk Drive You will want at least one 1.44MB 3$\frac{1}{2}$-inch floppy drive. Some older computers still have 5$\frac{1}{4}$-inch drives, but this size of floppy disk has been almost universally replaced by the 3$\frac{1}{2}$-inch floppy. Macintosh systems are equipped with 3$\frac{1}{2}$-inch drives.

How Are You Planning to Use Your System?

Although the selection of a computer system should take into account both business needs and personal preferences, the chart below will give you some idea of what to look for based on the anticipated use of your system.

Feature	Moderate Use System (basic word processing and spreadsheet use, small number of applications)	Heavy Use System (large databases or spreadsheets, extensive graphics applications, CAD)
Processor	486DX 66 MHz or Pentium 60 MHz Power Macintosh 6100 66 MHz or 7100 66 MHz	Pentium 90 or 100 MHz Power Macintosh 7100 80 MHz or 8100 100 MHz
RAM	8MB	16MB
Hard drive	350 to 500MB	1.0G

Purchasing a Notebook Computer

Notebook computers used to be almost exclusively considered a supplement to desktop computers. But today's notebook can nearly rival its desktop counterpart. The latest crop of notebook computers include Pentium-based models with jumbo hard disks as well as multimedia systems complete with an integrated CD-ROM and Sound Blaster Pro compatibility. Prices for these sleek new notebooks are steep—up to $7,500, but more affordable options also exist. When selecting a notebook system, there are a few other options to consider in addition to determining the processor, RAM, and hard disk you need.

~💻~

Weight When it comes to notebook computers, the lighter the better, unless carrying your notebook is part of your workout routine. Anything more than seven pounds is going to be very heavy if you need to carry it a long distance, for example, through the airport. Subnotebooks often weigh only about four pounds.

~💻~

Screen Type Screens in a notebook computer are different from a standard desktop computer. You have three basic choices when selecting a notebook computer, listed here in ascending order of price.

➡ Monochrome. A monochrome screen is a suitable choice if you are looking for an inexpensive notebook, most likely as a complement to your desktop system. If you don't do a lot of work with graphics and don't care about color, this is an economical choice.

➡ Dual-scan passive-matrix color. Passive color is the least expensive choice if you want a system that offers basic color.

➡ Active-matrix color. Active color provides more brightness and contrast but at a price. This is the most expensive option, but is worth it if you are planning to do on-screen presentations or work with a lot of color graphics.

~💻~

PCMCIA PCMCIA, which stands for Personal Computer Memory Card International Association, is the notebook computer expansion slot standard. PCMCIA slots allow you to use peripherals such as modems, external drives, tape backups, and sound cards with your notebook. To take advantage of the current and future options that PCMCIA (or a PC card) will provide, select a notebook with at least two PCMCIA slots.

Keyboard One of the common complaints about using a notebook computer is that the keyboard is awkward and difficult to use. Notebooks with traditional keyboards are usually easier to use if you plan to spend a lot of time working on your system.

Pointers If you are accustomed to a traditional mouse, working with a notebook's pointing device may take some getting used to. Today's notebook computers come with one of the following pointing devices:

- Integrated trackball
- Snap-on/clip-on trackball
- Integrated pointing stick
- Touchpad

Which pointing device works best is a matter of personal preference. Although the integrated trackball is currently the most common option, many users are beginning to indicate a preference for the pointing stick. The only way to truly know which device to choose is to try out some notebooks and see what is easiest for you.

Battery Life Battery life is an important consideration if you will be using your notebook for extended periods of time without access to recharging. Battery life in notebook computers ranges from a mere 1.5 hours to over 9 hours.

Where to Purchase Your System

If you are required to purchase your own computer system, there are three basic types of stores where you can purchase a computer once you have decided exactly what you need.

- Retail computer store
- Small independent store
- Mail-order store

Each option has advantages and disadvantages, but what's most important is to find a quality outlet that offers fair prices and good after-sale support.

Leading Computer Manufacturers

Here's a sample listing of top computer manufacturers and some of their products.

Name	Location	Phone	Product Line
Apple	Cupertino, CA	800-776-2333	Power Macintosh PowerBook notebooks
Dell	Austin, TX	800-289-3355	Desktop and notebook IBM-compatible computers
Gateway 2000	Sioux City, SD	800-846-2000	Desktop and notebook IBM-compatible computers
Toshiba	Irvine, CA	800-334-3445	Desktop and notebook IBM-compatible computers
Texas Instruments	Dallas, TX	800-TI-TEXAS	Desktop and notebook IBM-compatible computers
Power Computing	Austin, TX	800-999-7279	Macintosh clones
WinBook	Columbus, OH	800-468-2446	IBM-compatible notebook computers

Tips for Purchasing a Computer

- Have a written list of exactly what you need and don't stray from this list unless you have a compelling reason for doing so.

Comparison shop for prices, either by phone or by reading ads, before you set out to make your purchase.

Get a price quote in writing before making your purchase.

When purchasing a complete system make sure essential items haven't been omitted that will raise the final price.

Ask about warranties.

Find out what type of support the store or company provides if your computer doesn't work. Do you have to mail the system somewhere? Will they provide a loaner?

Before you make your hardware purchases you will probably want to add some peripheral devices (fax/modem, CD-ROM drive, tape backup, and so on) and software to your shopping list. The following chapters will help you determine your needs in these areas.

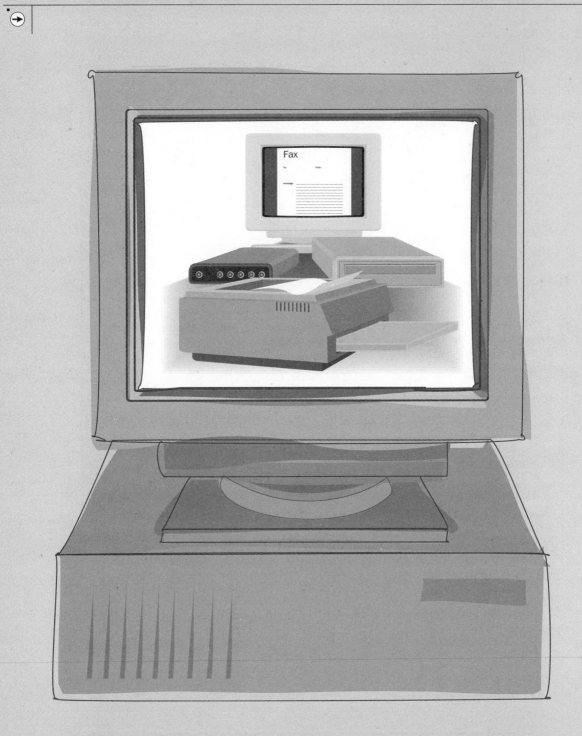

3

A *Practical* Guide to *Peripherals*

A fax/modem is an essential tool for any telecommuter. A modem is a device that allows you to send and receive data (both text and graphics) over telephone lines. Several years ago most modems didn't have faxing capability, but now that fax/modems are so inexpensive and predominate the modem marketplace, there's no reason not to include faxing capability with your modem. The fax/modem can't entirely replace a traditional fax machine, however. You still can't fax paper documents with a fax/modem, unless you scan the image into your system first.

Choosing a Fax/Modem

There are several things to take into consideration when you are looking for a fax/modem—its speed, the protocols it supports, and whether you prefer an internal or external model.

Modem speed is measured in bits per second or bps. The current standard in modems is 14,400 bps (also written as 14.4 Kbps), but within the next year 28.8 Kbps modems may have replaced this as the standard. Which speed should you opt for? If your basic need for telecommunications is to interface with traditional online services such as CompuServe and MCI Mail, you should do fine with a 14.4 Kbps fax/modem, since that is the fastest speed these services currently support in many locations. (Some online services have only reached 9,600 bps access.) If, however, you are going to transfer large amounts of data electronically, or send data over a LAN, a 28.8 Kbps modem will handle the job much faster. Just remember that you will need to have an equally fast modem on the other end to make this work.

V.32bis, V.34, V.42, V.42bis, V.FC—all of these modem protocols are very confusing for both novice and experienced computer users alike. Some refer to speed; others to varying modem standards. See the table on the next page for definitions of these protocols.

Your other main decision is whether to purchase an internal or external modem. There are distinct advantages to each option, as described below:

Internal Modem Advantages

➡   Traditionally less expensive than external modems

➔ Takes up less space

➔ Won't cause a serial port conflict with another device

External Modem Advantages

➔ Easier to install

➔ Can be used with more than one computer

➔ External controls let you know what the modem is doing.

Modem Protocols

The chart below will explain some of the terms you will encounter when purchasing a modem.

Protocol	Definition
V.32bis	Operates at a top speed of 14,000 bps
V.32terbo	Operates at a top speed of 19,200 bps
V.34 (or V.FC)	Operates at a top speed of 28,800 bps
V.42	Error control standard
V.42bis	Data compression standard

The Fax/Modem of the Future Tomorrow's modems will offer even more advanced features that can increase a telecommuter's productivity. You can look forward to the following technologies:

➔ VoiceView (developed by Radish Communications, Microsoft, and Hayes) allows users on a voice telephone call to switch to data mode to send a text message or graphic image to the person on the other line, and then switch back to the voice call.

➔ Voice/Data Switching Technology allows alternate use of voice and data communication on a single telephone line.

DSVD (Digital Simultaneous Voice and Data) Modems are V.34 class (28.8 Kbps) modems that allow you to share voice and data at the same time over one phone line.

 Voice Record and Playback permits your modem and computer system to act as a voice mail center.

More Information on Fax/Modems Online services also offer an abundance of information on fax/modems. Here's a list of suggested places to go on the most popular online services:

America Online

 Global Village Communication Forum (Keyword: Global)

 Macintosh Communications Forum (Keyword: MCM)

 PC Telecommunications & Networking Forum (Keyword: PC Telecom)

CompuServe

 Hayes Forum (GO HAYFORUM)

 Macintosh Communications Forum (GO MACCOMM)

 Modem Vendor Forum (GO MODEMVENDOR) offers support from the following vendors: Boca Research, Global Village Communication, US Robotics

 PC Communications Forum (GO PCCOM)

GEnie

 BBS and Telecommunications RoundTable (BBS)

 Hayes RoundTable (HAYES)

 IBM Support RoundTable (IBMSUPPORT)

Prodigy

 Computer Bulletin Board (JUMP: COMPUTER BB)

 Global Village Communication (JUMP: GLOBAL)

Suggested Products

All of the products listed below are Hayes-compatible and support V.42 error control and V.42bis data compression as well as the appropriate protocol (V.34, V.FC, or V.32bis) for their speed.

Manufacturer	Products
Hayes Microcomputer Products P.O. Box 105203 Atlanta, GA 30348 404-441-1617	Internal and external modems for PC and Macintosh. Most include Smartcom software. **Hayes OPTIMA 288 V.FC + FAX Modem** ($579). 22.8 Kbps modem suitable for fast data transfer over a LAN at a speed of more than 1MB per minute. **Hayes ACCURA 288 V.34/V.FC + fax Modem** ($299). Traditional 28.8 Kbps modem. **Hayes OPTIMA Modems for PCMCIA with EZJack.** 28.8 Kbps ($579) and 14.4 Kbps ($279) notebook modems with pop-out RJ-11 connector.
U.S. Robotics 7770 North Frontage Road Skokie, IL 60077-2690 800-342-5877	Internal and external fax/modems for both PC and Macintosh computers. Most include QuickLink II data/fax software. **Sportster High Speed Data/Fax.** Offers both 28.8 Kbps ($329 internal/$349 external) and 14.4 Kbps ($129 internal/$159 external) PC modems. **Mac & Fax Sportster.** Offers both 28.8 Kbps ($369) and 14.4 Kbps ($159) external Mac modems. **Sportster Data/Fax PCMCIA 2.1.** 28.8 Kbps ($499) and 14.4 Kbps ($259) notebook modems with dual RJ-11 connector. **Courier Dual Standard Data/Fax PCMCIA.** High-speed 28.8 Kbps ($575) and 14.4 Kbps ($499) notebook modems; automatically connects with other modems at their highest speed. **Courier High Speed.** Offers several options for high-speed modems that automatically connect with other modems at their highest speed.

Suggested Products (Continued)

All of the products listed below are Hayes-compatible and support V.42 error control and V.42bis data compression as well as the appropriate protocol (V.34, V.FC, or V.32bis) for their speed.

Manufacturer	Products
Global Village Communication 1144 East Arques Avenue Sunnyvale, CA 94086 800-736-4821	Fax/modems for Macintosh computers. Includes GlobalFAX software. **Teleport Series.** Offers 28.8 Kbps, 19.2 Kbps, and 14.4 Kbps fax/modems for desktop computers. **PowerPort Series.** Offers 28.8 Kbps, 19.2 Kbps and 14.4 Kbps fax/modems for PowerBook notebook computers.
Boca Research 1377 Clint Moore Road Boca Raton, FL 33487-2722 407-997-6227	Internal and external fax/modems for PC and Macintosh. Includes FaxWorks (PC) and QuickLink (Mac) software. **BOCAMODEM** ($199 internal/$249 external). Traditional 28.8 Kbps fax/modem. **SoundExpression 14.4VSp** ($179). 14.4 Kbps modem offering voice mail, speakerphone, fax-on-demand support, and a CD-ROM interface. **Multimedia Voice Modem** ($245). 14.4 Kpbs modem offering voice mail and fax-on-demand capabilities. **Data/Fax BOCAMODEM.** Traditional 14.4 Kbps fax/modem. **BOCAMODEM** ($369). A 14.4 Kbps modem for notebook computers.

Selecting a Printer

With quality laser printers now selling for less than $400, there's really no reason to select a dot-matrix printer anymore. One major choice in a laser printer is the resolution. Should you choose a 300 dpi (dots per inch) printer, or one that prints 600 dpi? The 600 dpi model will give you better quality and is a better choice if you will be printing a lot of graphic images or presentations. But if you mostly print basic word processing or spreadsheet documents, a 300 dpi printer will still give you a quality laser output. Pages per minute (PPM) on a home office laser printer vary, so if speed is important this is one area to consider.

Ink-jet printers are another affordable option for the home office, particularly if you want color printing (most ink jets now include this option) and don't care if your final output isn't true laser quality. In fact, the output of most quality ink-jet printers is very close to the output of a 300 dpi laser printer. The main choice in color output in an ink-jet printer is between three-color and four-color printing. Four-color produces the best quality, since it also includes a black cartridge, which makes printing black-and-white documents easier.

More Information on Printers For printer information and support, try the following areas on these popular online services:

America Online

   Macintosh Hardware Forum (Keyword: MHW)

   PC Hardware Forum (Keyword: PC Hardware)

CompuServe

   HP Peripherals (GO HPPER)

   Macintosh Hardware (GO MACHW)

   PC Hardware (GO PCHW)

   Canon Forum (GO CANON)

GEnie

   IBM PC RoundTable (IBMPC)

Macintosh RoundTable (MAC)

Prodigy

 Computer Bulletin Board (JUMP: COMPUTER BB)

Hardware Support Bulletin Board (JUMP: HARDWARE BB).

Suggested Products

The printers listed below will give you a good idea of what's available for the home office market at about $1,000 or less

Manufacturer	Products
Apple Computer 20525 Mariani Avenue Cupertino, CA 95014 800-538-9696	**Color StyleWriter 2400** ($525) and **Color StyleWriter Pro** ($629). Color ink-jet printers for the Macintosh. **Portable StyleWriter** ($439). Lightweight ink-jet printer for use with the PowerBook notebook computer. **Personal LaserWriter 300** ($689). 4 PPM 300 dpi Macintosh laser printer. **Personal LaserWriter 320** ($959). PostScript Macintosh laser printer.
Brother International Corporation 200 Cottontail Lane Somerset , NJ 08875-6714 800-276-7746	**HL-630** ($399) and **HL-645** ($499). 6 PPM 300 dpi PC laser printers. **HL-655M** ($599). 6 PPM 300 dpi PC and Macintosh laser printer. **HL-660** ($699). 6 PPM 600 dpi PC laser printer. **MFC-4500ML** ($999). A 5-in-1 multifunction product (laser printer/fax/copier/scanner/fax modem). **MFC-4000ML** ($899). A 3-in-1 multifunction product (laser printer/fax/copier).

Suggested Products (Continued)

The printers listed below will give you a good idea of what's available for the home office market at about $1,000 or less

Manufacturer	Products
Hewlett-Packard Company Direct Marketing Organization P.O. Box 58059, MS511L-SJ Santa Clara, CA 95051-8059 800-752-0900	**HP DeskJet 540** for the PC and **DeskWriter 540** for the Macintosh ($365). Monochrome ink-jet printers with color upgrade kit ($49). **HP DeskJet 660C** for the PC and **DeskWriter 660C** for the Macintosh ($499). Color ink-jet printers. **HP DeskJet 320** for the notebook PC and **DeskWriter 320** for the Macintosh PowerBook ($379). Ink-jet printer with color upgrade kit ($49). **HP LaserJet 5P** ($1,109). 6 PPM 600 dpi PC laser printer with built-in infrared technology for wireless printing. **HP LaserJet 4L** ($650). 4 PPM 300 dpi PC laser printer.
Canon Computer Systems 2995 Redhill Avenue Costa Mesa, CA 92626 800-848-4123	**BJ-100** ($249) and **BJ-200e** ($299). Bubble Jet monochrome ink-jet printers. **BJC-4000** ($549) and **BJC-600** ($579). Four-color ink-jet printers.

Do You Need a CD-ROM Drive?

Several years ago a CD-ROM drive was a luxury item, purchased by multimedia fans and computer gamers. Today it's become a computer system staple, one that few telecommuters really can afford to do without. Here are eight reasons for buying a CD-ROM drive:

 A CD-ROM encyclopedia takes up less space than its paper-bound counterpart.

➡ You can look up phone numbers throughout the country on one CD.

➡ Many popular software packages now come on CD.

➡ Many books include a CD with related software.

➡ Many computer training programs are on CD.

➡ Buying a shareware CD is less expensive and time-consuming than down-loading shareware from online services.

➡ You can use it after hours; there are many game, entertainment, and family education programs on CD.

➡ CD-ROMs are now less expensive than ever.

Selecting a CD-ROM Drive If you are purchasing a new desktop computer and want a CD-ROM drive you can buy a "multimedia system" that will contain all the hardware and software necessary to run CD-ROM titles. Most of these systems will include the following:

➡ 2X or 4X CD-ROM drive

➡ 16- or 32-bit sound card

➡ Stereo speakers

➡ Bundled CD-ROM titles

If you already own a PC-compatible computer and want to add multimedia capabilities, you will need to purchase an upgrade kit that includes the items listed above. Unless you are skilled in installing both computer hardware and software, you will also need to pay an installation charge.

The main decision you will have to make in choosing a CD-ROM drive is whether to purchase a double-speed (2X) or quadruple-speed (4X) drive, the two most common speeds curently sold. A double speed drive accesses data at approximately 320ms (milliseconds) and can transfer about 300K of data per second. A quad-speed drive accesses data in only 195ms and is capable of 600K per second data transfer. Quad speed is the fastest option, and is more expensive, but it will soon become the CD-ROM standard. PC users should also be sure that their drive is MPC (Multimedia PC) compliant, which means that it meets standard CD-ROM specifications. Internal Mac CD-ROM drives should already meet these standards.

~▭~

More Information on CD-ROMs If you're interested in getting more details about CD-ROM and multimedia technology, look for the following:

   How Multimedia Works, by Erik Holsinger. 1994, Ziff-Davis Press.

Online services have a lot of information about CD-ROM drives and titles as well as multimedia. Some suggestions:

America Online

   Macintosh Multimedia (Keyword: MMM)

   PC Multimedia Forum (Keyword: PC Multimedia)

CompuServe

   CD-ROM Forum (GO CDROM)

   CD-ROM Vendors A Forum (GO CDVEN)

   CDROM Vendors B Forum (GO CDVENB)

   Creative Labs Forum (GO BLASTER)

   Macintosh Multimedia Forum (GO MACMULTI)

   Media Vision Forum (GO MEDIAVISION)

   Multimedia A Vendor Forum (GO MULTIVEN)

   Multimedia B Vendor Forum (GO MULTIBVEN)

   Multimedia C Vendor Forum (GO MULTICVEN)

   Multimedia Forum (GO MULTIMEDIA)

GEnie

   Multimedia, Desktop Video, and Virtual Reality RoundTable (CYBERSPACE)

Prodigy

➡ Computer Bulletin Board (JUMP: COMPUTER BB)

➡ Hardware Support Bulletin Board (JUMP: HARDWARE BB)

Determining Your Data Backup Needs

Once you begin telecommuting, you will start storing important business documents on your home computer system. Many companies already have a backup strategy in place for its home-based employees, for example, backing up to a network drive. But in some cases you may be responsible for your own backup system.

You need to make two main decisions before selecting a tape backup system: determining the amount of data you need to back up (both now and in the future) and choosing either an internal or external model. Although internal tape backup systems are generally less expensive than their external counterparts and take up less space, an external system is the best solution for users who need to back up more than one computer, for example, a desktop and a notebook system. The latest backup systems suitable for home office use can store up to 1G per tape or cartridge using data compression, which should easily fit most users' data on a single tape.

Backing up your data on recordable CD is another option, although currently more expensive than tape backup systems. A recordable CD (CD-R) drive offers the advantage of random access, increased speed, and the ability to function as a CD-ROM player, recorder, and backup system in one unit. Look for these systems to drop in price in the future.

~🖥~

Backup Strategies in the Home Office In general, most hard disks are reasonably reliable. I've never had one crash in the seven years I've had a home office. But there's always a first time, and that's why developing a backup strategy *now* is so crucial. Some of the many potential computer data disasters:

➡ You can accidentally delete important files.

➡ Important files can become corrupted.

Your hard disk can stop functioning or "crash."

 An accident or natural disaster can destroy or damage your computer system.

To be prepared if a computer disaster should strike, here's a sample home office backup strategy:

 Make two complete backups and store one off-site.

 Back up all revised data once a week, rotating two tapes, keeping one off-site.

 Make new complete backups every month or so, or whenever you make major changes to your system.

 Store critical files on a floppy disk on a daily basis.

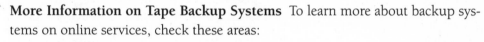

More Information on Tape Backup Systems To learn more about backup systems on online services, check these areas:

America Online

 PC Hardware Forum (Keyword: PC Hardware)

Macintosh Hardware Forum (Keyword: MHW)

CompuServe

Macintosh Hardware (GO MACHW)

PC Hardware (GO PCHW)

GEnie

IBM PC RoundTable (IBMPC)

Macintosh RoundTable (MAC)

Prodigy

Hardware Support BB (JUMP: HARDWARE BB)

Suggested Products

The backup systems listed below are options for your home office.

Manufacturer	Products
Conner Peripherals 3081 Zanker Road San Jose, CA 95134 800-4-CONNER	Tape*Stor products includes Backup Exec for DOS and Windows software. Data cartridge drives are suitable for either PC or Macintosh backups. **Tape*Stor 420** ($199 internal/$369 external) mini-cartridge system stores 420MB. **Tape*Stor 850** ($349 internal/ $529 external) minicartridge system stores 850MB of data. **Data Cartridge 2150** ($489 internal/$ $689 external), a SCSI tape drive that stores 250MB of data. **Data Cartridge 2525** ($649 internal/ $889 external), a SCSI drive that stores 525 MB of data.
Creative Labs 1901 McCarthy Boulevard Milpitas, CA 95935 800-998-5227	Digital Edge CD-R recordable CD system can store up to 650MB on a single disc. To be released mid-1995 at a retail price of less than $2,000.
Hewlett-Packard Colorado Memory Systems 800 South Taft Avenue Loveland, CO 80537 800-845-7905	Includes Colorado Backup for DOS and Colorado Backup for Windows software. **Colorado Trakker 700** ($479), an external parallel port backup system with a storage capacity up to 680MB. **Jumbo 1400** ($429), a minicartridge QIC-3020-MC tape backup system that stores up to 1.36G using data compression. **HP Colorado T1000** ($239), an internal mini-cartridge backup system storing up to 800MB.

Suggested Products (Continued)

The backup systems listed below are options for your home office.

Manufacturer	Products
Mountain Network Solutions 360 El Pueblo Road Scotts Valley, CA 95066-4268 408-438-6650	Includes FileSafe First for Windows backup and disaster recovery software. **FileSafe SideCar II** ($475), a parallel port tape backup system for desktop PCs and notebook computers that stores up to 305MB on a DC2120 cartridge. **FileSafe TD-350** ($229), an internal minicartridge tape drive that stores 350MB. **FileSafe TD-700** ($399), an internal QIC-3010 tape drives that stores up to 700MB on a minicartridge. **Personal DAT** ($1,399 internal and $1,699 external) stores up to 4G of compressed data.
Pinnacle Micro 19 Technology Irvine, CA 92718 800-553-7070	**RCD-1000** ($1,995), a recordable CD backup system that stores up to 680MB of data. Includes backup software for Windows or Macintosh.

4

Communications Software for Telecommuters

You will need data communications software to connect your computer (via its modem) to any outside computer system or service. Many online services have their own required communications software, such as America Online and Prodigy, and others, such as CompuServe, have optional interface programs. But to connect to most other services and BBSs as well as many mainframe computer systems, you will need a general-purpose data communications program. Many of these programs now include fax sending and receiving capabilities that utilize the faxing ability of your fax/modem. Independent fax software is also available.

Selecting Data Communications Software

Most data communications programs offer the following basic features:

 Ability to view, upload, and download data

 Dialing directories in which you can store the numbers and settings of any service you call

 Online capture feature which allows you to log your entire online session in a text file

 Back-scroll buffer offering the ability to capture a certain amount of the data that has already displayed on your screen

 Chat mode that creates two windows when you're participating in an online conference to differentiate the messages you send from the ones you receive

What else should you look for in communications software? A lot depends on your personal preferences, but here are some basic things to consider when selecting a communications program:

 File transfer capabilities. A file transfer protocol is a set of rules that governs the transferring of data across computer systems. A protocol will predetermine such things as block size and the method of error correction used. Common file transfer protocols include Xmodem, Kermit, and Zmodem. Xmodem and Kermit were once popular, but Zmodem is currently a faster protocol. CompuServe has its own file transfer protocol, called CompuServe B, which you should use when downloading and uploading files to this system.

→ *Terminal emulation support.* This feature allows your computer system to emulate, or behave, as if it were a terminal attached to a remote system. The proper terminal emulation can be important when logging into remote mainframe systems.

→ *Predefined access to major online services.* If you regularly connect with services such as MCI Mail, CompuServe, GEnie, Dow Jones, or others, you may prefer a communications package that is already set up to access these services.

→ *Integration with fax software.* Although you can use two separate programs for communications and faxing, it really doesn't make sense to do so. Look for a package that can handle both functions.

→ *GIF viewer.* Allows you to view a GIF file as you download it. GIF is the most common format used for both photo and graphic images.

→ *Script files.* A script file performs the steps needed to log on to another computer system, including the user ID, password, and other commands you would manually enter.

→ *Customizability.* The best communications programs offer complete customizability so that you can define toolbars and dialing directories to your specifications.

→ Modifying Port Settings

Your communications program will most likely include default settings for each new entry in the dialing directory. In many cases, this will work fine, but if your online service calls for settings that are different from the default, or if you have difficulty connecting to a particular service, you will need to change these settings. These port settings include:

Parity. Specifies the type of parity checking to perform. Choices include None, Odd, Even, Mark, and Space.

➔ Modifying Port Settings (Continued)

Data bits. Specifies the number of data bits. Options include 7 or 8 data bits.

Stop bits. Specifies the number of stop bits. Choices are 1 or 2 stop bits.

Duplex (echo). Determines whether or not the characters you type will echo on the screen. Options include full duplex (characters don't echo) and half duplex (characters do echo). If every character you type appears twice, you should reset to full; if you can't see what you type, reset to half.

The standard default settings are

➔ Parity: None

➔ Data bits: 8

➔ Stop bits: 1

➔ Duplex: Full

These settings will work in most instances, but certain online services, such as CompuServe and GEnie, require E-7-1 (Parity: Even, Data bits: 7, and Stop bits: 1) settings. And GEnie requires half duplex, rather than full.

Selecting Fax Software

All fax programs provide the basic features for sending, receiving, and storing faxes, but depending on your specific requirements, you may want more sophisticated fax capabilities, including the following:

 Fax creation. Cover pages are an important aspect of creating a fax, and the best products offer many possible cover sheets from which to choose, including the option to modify or create your own. The ability to place graphic images in your faxes such as logos, letterhead, and scanned signatures can also be an important feature. Some full-featured programs allow the use of a separate second page and include a fax spell-checker.

➡ *Fax sending.* The ability to send a fax directly from another application is an important feature if you plan to fax a lot of documents created in your word processing software. You will also want the ability to preview your fax before sending, print in the background, send to multiple recipients, and set a specific time to send your faxes in order to take advantage of lower phone rates during non-business hours.

➡ *Fax phone book.* The phone book is where you store your recipients' fax numbers, and is similar to the phone book of a communications program. If you already have a contact or address list in another application, the ability to import and export data will be a time-saving advantage. Using a compatible communications program will allow you to create one list for both data and fax calls.

➡ *OCR.* OCR (optical character recognition) will allow you to convert your faxes into editable text documents.

➡ *Fax management tools.* If you send or receive a large number of faxes, the ability to organize and manage your faxes can become very important. Send and receive logs and search capabilities are recommended features.

➡ *Fax printing.* Most fax software now includes an option for printing faxes as you receive them, allowing your computer and software to simulate a real fax machine. More advanced programs allow you to print only selected areas or specific pages and can print in the background.

➡ Faxing with Windows 95

Windows 95, scheduled for release in August 1995, includes the Microsoft At Work Fax (AWFax) application that is currently part of Windows for Workgroups 3.11. AWFax will offer fax sending and receiving capabilities, four sample cover pages, and an address book. Windows 95 also includes a 32-bit "light" version of HyperTerminal data communications software. If you want basic data and fax communication capabilities and are planning to use Windows 95, AWFax and HyperTerminal may be all you need, but for more sophisticated options you will still want a third party program.

Suggested Programs

Once you have decided what you are looking for in data and fax communications programs, it's time to start comparing the features of different products. Listed here are some quality communications programs and their best features.

~🖥~

DATASTORM PROCOMM PLUS 2.0 for Windows

→ Provides predefined links to CompuServe and MCI Mail

→ Supports Zmodem, Kermit, Xmodem, 1K-Xmodem, 1 K-Xmodem-g, Ymodem, Ymodem-g, CIS-B+, ASCII, RAW ASCII, and IND$FILE file transfer protocols

→ Supports the following terminal emulations: ADDS 60, ADDS 90, ADM 31, ADM 3A, ADM 5, ANSI, ATT 4410, ATT 605, DG D100, DG D200, DG D210, ESPIRIT 3, HEATH 19, IBM 3101, IBM 3161, IBM 3270, IBM PC, TTY, TVI 910, TVI 912, TVI 920, TVI 922, TVI 925, TVI 950, TVI 955, VIDTEX, VT-52, VT-100, VT-102, VT-220, VT-320, WYSE 50, WYSE 75, and WYSE 100

→ Offers a GIF Viewer

→ Customizable Action Bars

→ Features the Windows ASPECT script language

→ Retail price: $179

~🖥~

Delrina Communications Suite (Windows Data/Fax Communications Software) This suite includes WinComm PRO 1.1 and WinFax PRO 4.0, both of which can also be purchased separately. The Communications Suite also includes Fax Mailbox, a fax receiving service, and Fax Broadcast, which enables users to broadcast a fax to up to 10,000 recipients in one call. A Macintosh version will soon be available. Delrina WinComm PRO 1.1

→ Offers pre-defined links to CompuServe, MCI Mail, GEnie, BIX, Delphi, NewsNet, Dow Jones, and AT&T Mail

➔ Supports Zmodem, Xmodem, Ymodem, CompuServe B+, and Kermit file transfer protocols

➔ Includes HyperGuard virus detector that detects viruses as you download files

➔ Supports the following terminal emulations: ANSI, TTY, VT-52, VT-102, VT-220, VT-320, IBM3101, IBM3278, and CompuServe

➔ Offers a GIF Viewer

➔ Includes the Delrina Internet Messenger which allows you to easily send, receive, and organize Internet e-mail.

➔ Offers automatic Internet registration through a variety of service providers

➔ Customizable Button Bars and phone books

➔ Scripting language includes an Application Programming Interface (API) compatible with programming languages such as Visual Basic or C++

➔ Retail price: $129 ($179 for the entire Suite)

WinFax PRO 4.0 (Windows Fax Software)

➔ Faxes directly from Windows applications

➔ Includes 101 sample cover pages

➔ Fax Autoforwarding allows users to forward received faxes to another destination

➔ Includes Fax-a-File, enabling users to send actual documents rather than just a fax image

➔ Provides ability to send e-mail via cc:Mail or Microsoft Mail

➔ Can modify faxes with annotation tools similar to those found in paint programs

➔ Includes fax spell-checker

➔ OCR technology can convert fax images to editable text files

➔ Retail price: $129 ($179 for the entire suite)

Global Village Communication FaxWorks PRO 3.0 (Windows Fax Software)

➡ Includes ability to combine pages from multiple Windows applications into one fax

➡ Can print incoming faxes directly to printer

➡ Imports phone book data from Act!, Lotus Organizer, PackRat, and dBASE III/IV

➡ OCR capability converts faxes to editable text

➡ Supports HP ScanJet, The Complete PC, Fujitsu, and TWAIN compatible scanners

➡ Includes sophisticated FaxTracker to simplify fax management

➡ Compresses faxes up to 75 percent to reduce required disk space

➡ Retail price: $129

Global Village Communication GlobalFax Software 2.5 (Macintosh Fax Software)

➡ Offers ability to fax from any Macintosh application

➡ Can group multiple documents from different applications into one fax transmission

➡ Works with GlobalFax OCR (sold separately)

➡ Provides ability to use up to three different calling cards to place fax calls

➡ Can fax from different area codes without making changes in phone book

➡ Included with Global Village modems, not sold separately

Hayes Smartcom Data/FAX Pro (Windows Data/Fax Communications Software)

 Supports data speeds up to 230,400 bits to take advantage of the capabilities of 28.8 Kbps modems

➡ Offers GIF viewer

➡ Features SCOPE (Simple Communications Programming Environment), a scripting language that can automatically create a script based on the keystrokes you enter

➡ Provides directory from other applications

➡ Converts faxes into text with OCR technology

➡ Supports Zmodem, Kermit, and CompuServe B Plus, as well as all variations on Xmodem and Ymodem

➡ Supports TTY, ANSI.SYS, VT52, VT100/102, VT220, VT320, Prestel, and Teletel terminal emulation

➡ Offers fax broadcasting and scheduling

➡ Retail price: $79

Hayes Smartcom II for Macintosh (Macintosh Communications Software)

 Offers TTY, VT52, 100/102,230, ANSI, Prestel, and Minitel terminal emulation support

 Features Interactive Graphics, allowing the real-time exchange of graphic files

➡ Autopilot scripting language automatically creates a script based on the keystrokes you enter

 Offers floating keypad windows to provide point-and-click access to extended keyboard functions for PowerBook users

 Includes English, French, and German language versions

➡ Retail price: $149

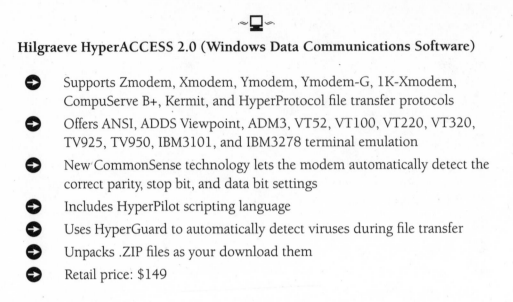

Hilgraeve HyperACCESS 2.0 (Windows Data Communications Software)

➡ Supports Zmodem, Xmodem, Ymodem, Ymodem-G, 1K-Xmodem, CompuServe B+, Kermit, and HyperProtocol file transfer protocols

➡ Offers ANSI, ADDS Viewpoint, ADM3, VT52, VT100, VT220, VT320, TV925, TV950, IBM3101, and IBM3278 terminal emulation

➡ New CommonSense technology lets the modem automatically detect the correct parity, stop bit, and data bit settings

➡ Includes HyperPilot scripting language

➡ Uses HyperGuard to automatically detect viruses during file transfer

➡ Unpacks .ZIP files as your download them

➡ Retail price: $149

Mustang QModemPro (Windows Data/Fax Communications Software)

➡ Supports ASCII, Xmodem, Xmodem/CRC, 1K Xmodem, 1K Xmodem/G, Ymodem (batch), Ymodem/G (batch), Zmodem (batch), Kermit, and CompuServe B Plus file transfer protocols

➡ Supports ADDS VP60, ADM 3A, ANSI, Avatar, DG 100, DG 200, DG 210, Doorway, Hazeltine 1500, Heath 19, IBM 3101, RIPscrip, TTY, TV1910, TV1912, TV1920, TV1922, TV1925, TV1950, TV1955, Vidtex, VT52, VT100, VT102, VT220, VT320, Wyse 30, Wyse 60, Wyse 85, Wyse 100, and Wyse 185 terminal emulations

➡ Includes built-in GIF file viewer

➡ Host mode allows users to create their own mini-BBS

➡ Can fax directly from other Windows applications

➡ Includes Script Language Interface for QmodemPro (SLIQ), based on the BASIC language

➡ Retail price: $139

~□~

Software Ventures MicroPhone Pro 2.1.1 (Macintosh Data/Fax Communications Software)

➡ Includes version for both Power Macintosh and 68000-series Macs

➡ Includes Internet tools to make connecting to the Internet easier

➡ Offers the ability to have multiple concurrent sessions

➡ Loran, an electronic mail front end, simplifies mail exchanges on multiple online services

➡ Supports ASCII, Xmodem, Ymodem, Ymodem-g, Zmodem, Kermit, MacTerminal 1.1 and CompuServe B Plus file transfer protocols

➡ Terminal emulation includes TTY, VT52, VT100, VT102, VT220, VT320, Wyse 50, and PC ANSI

➡ Includes STartFaxing software to send, receive, and manage faxes

➡ Also offers similar Windows version, MicroPhone Pro for Windows

➡ Retail price: $195

Vendor Information

Manufacturer	Address	Phone
DATASTORM	P.O. Box 1471 Columbia, MO 65205	314-443-3282
Delrina	6320 San Ignacio Avenue San Jose, CA 95119-1209	800-268-6082
Global Village Communication	1144 East Arques Avenue Sunnyvale, CA 94086	800-736-4821
Hayes	P.O. Box 105203 Atlanta, GA 30348	404-441-1617
Hilgraeve	Genesis Center 111 Conant Avenue Monroe, MI 48161	800-826-2760

Vendor Information (Continued)

Manufacturer	Address	Phone
Mustang Software	P.O. Box 2264 Bakersfield, CA 93303	805-873-2500
Software Ventures	2907 Claremont Avenue Berkeley, CA 94705	800-336-6477

More Information on Communications/Fax Software

Online services also offer an abundance of information on fax/modems. Here's a list of suggested places to go on the most popular online services:

America Online

- Global Village Communication Forum (Keyword: Global)
- Macintosh Communications Forum (Keyword: MCM)
- PC Telecommunications & Networking Forum (Keyword: PC Telecom)

CompuServe

- Crosstalk Forum (GO XTALK)
- Delrina Forum (GO DELRINA)
- Hayes Forum (GO HAYFORUM)
- Macintosh Communications Forum (GO MACCOMM)
- Modem Vendor Forum (GO MODEMVENDOR) offers support for Global Village Communication products
- PC Communications Forum (GO PCCOM)
- PC Vendor A Forum (GO PCVENA) for support on Mustang Software
- The DATASTORM Forum (GO DATAST)

GEnie

- BBS and Telecommunications RoundTable (BBS)

Hayes RoundTable (HAYES)

 IBM Support RoundTable (IBMSUPPORT)

5 Remote *Access* to Office *Computers* and *Networks*

If you are a part-time telecommuter, travel frequently from your home base, or use both a desktop and notebook computer, you will soon realize the difficulties that arise from working on more than one computer system. Not only do you have to remember what information is on which system, but you may often find that the important data you need is on another computer, possibly thousands of miles away. Remote access technology can provide a solution to these problems. Remote access is predicted to grow rapidly over the next few years and the technological advances in this area will greatly benefit telecommuters and mobile workers.

There are basically two ways to access other computers from remote locations. Remote control software is one means of connecting to a distant computer or network. Remote node technology is another way of providing users with access to remote networks. What is the difference between remote control and remote node? Using remote control, applications run on the host (distant) computer and users can connect to either a standalone computer or a network. Remote node technology, however, allows a remote computer (the computer you're currently using) to function as a network workstation with applications running on that remote system. If you will frequently use remote access to retrieve data and control faraway computers, you will probably want to invest in a second telephone line, reserving one for voice and the other for data/fax communications. A computer-literate end user can set up and operate remote control software; remote node technology requires the expertise of the computer support staff. In many companies both remote control and remote node technology are used to provide an overall solution to remote access. Which option is best for you depends on your specific computing needs and the hardware and software you have available. Each method has its benefits.

Remote Control

- Is a good choice for accessing large databases or spreadsheets since processing is done on the host computer
- Allows mobile users to access software they can't have on their mobile system due to power or disk space limitations (however, you need to be careful of the cost of long distance phone calls)
- Offers an inexpensive option for a single user or small number of users

Remote Node

 Is the best solution for client/server technology or group scheduling programs

→ Is more cost-effective for a larger number of users

→ Works better with Windows applications

Using Remote Control Software

Remote control software allows you to do many things:

 Access and retrieve data on a remote computer via modem

→ Access your primary computer from your notebook system at a remote location

→ Provide technical support and/or training to a remote user

→ Transfer files from one computer to another

→ Demonstrate products remotely

→ Automate manual file retrieval at off hours

→ Allow multiple users in varying locations to collaborate on one project

Only a few years ago most remote control programs were relatively slow, difficult to use, and didn't work well with Windows. But recent versions have resolved these former problems considerably, resulting in new software that greatly benefits telecommuters. How does remote control software work?

Let's say you are working at home and want to reach your desktop computer at the office. With remote control software and a modem installed on both systems, you can call your office computer, (termed the host computer in this instance), from your home computer (referred to as the remote or viewer computer). You will then have access to the files and data on the office computer, even though you haven't left home. With remote control software you can access standalone computers as well as LANs, if your particular product supports network access.

What should you look for in remote control software? Here are some suggestions (followed by some suggested programs):

➡ *Speed*   Remote control software used to be notoriously slow, particularly with Windows applications. A program that uses data compression and can utilize high-speed modems will provide you faster access.

➡ *Ease of installation and use*   Nontechnical users will benefit greatly from a program that offers automatic installation and is intuitive to use.

➡ *Security*   Security is especially important with the recent proliferation of computer thieves and hackers. Features such as virus scanners, password protection, access restrictions, and host callback will help ensure you are working with clean data as well as keep intruders off your system. Call-back security, in which the host computer calls back the remote computer at a predesignated phone number, also has the advantage of placing the cost of the call on the host computer location. Roving call-back is useful to mobile computer users since it allows you to enter your current callback number rather than dialing a predetermined one.

➡ *File synchronization*   One of the problems of working with multiple computer systems is the possibility of having the current version of a particular file or document on one system and an earlier version on another system. File synchronization can solve this problem by automatically ensuring that the latest version is on both the host and remote computers. File synchronization is a feature of most of the programs suggested below, but you can also purchase a specialized file synchronization utility such as LinkPro's PowerSync.

Farallon Timbuktu Pro for Macintosh

➡ Allows transfer of files between Macs and PCs

➡ Background file exchange allows users to work on other tasks while transferring files

➡ Security features include password and privilege restrictions

➡ Multiple host/multiple guest feature allows simultaneous connections

➔ Timbuktu for Windows also available

➔ Retail price: $199

Microcom Carbon Copy 2.5 for Windows

➔ Includes terminal emulation capabilities

➔ Security features include password protection and both traditional and roving callback

➔ Offers Software Gateway for access to networked computers via one modem

➔ Retail price: $199

 Carbon Copy offers several remote control options

Norton-Lambert Close-Up 6.0 for Windows/DOS

➔ Includes Expert System technology to automatically configure Close-Up on the user's system

➔ Allows the Host modem to be used for both remote communications and faxing

➔ Includes multilevel password, stationary callback, and roving callback security

- Allows simultaneous remote printing in Windows and DOS
- Non-Intrusive Technology allows Windows to continue running at optimal levels
- Includes virus checker
- Retail price: $199

Stac ReachOut Remote Control 4.02 (Modem and LAN versions for Windows/DOS)

- Security features include intruder guard, log-in notification, and password with callback
- Does not modify your Windows system files
- Provides automatic virus detection
- Offers drive-mapping capabilities with the included ReachOut Remote Access software
- Retail price: $199

Symantec Norton pcANYWHERE 2.0 for Windows

- Enhanced Windows support, including Windows 95
- Smart Setup automatically detects system configuration
- TCP/IP support allows for faster access to LANs
- Provides automatic file synchronization
- Security features include password, encryption, drive access restrictions, and host screen disable
- Retail price: $199

Traveling Software Laplink for Windows

- SmartXchange feature offers automatic file synchronization
- Includes serial and parallel cables for direct file transfer capabilities
- SpeedSync technology allows faster updates by sending only file changes rather than complete files

Configuration is easier in the latest remote control products

ReachOut Configuration
File   DOS Configuration   Help

Communications

COM Port   Setup

Remote Access

☐ Client
☐ Server

☑ Adv Options

Computer Name

Patrice   ☐ Use Default Name

EXIT   DOS Config   ? Help

➤ Includes password protection and callback restriction security

➤ Also offers Laplink Wireless for Windows for wireless access

➤ Retail price: $199.95

Triton Technologies CoSession for Windows 2.0

➤ Supports multiple simultaneous remote connections

➤ Setup provides automatic COM port detection and baud rate

➤ Offers remote control and remote access capabilities

➤ Supports both Windows and DOS applications

➤ Retail price: $199

With Laplink, you can access a remote network workstation

Using Remote Node Technology

The technical details of comparison features on remote node products are something that will interest a network guru more than a typical end user. Listed below are some highly regarded remote node systems, which can provide network dial-in to DOS, Windows, Macintosh, and UNIX users.

- Shiva LanRover products
- Microcom LANexpress
- Telebit NetBlazer series
- Farallon Timbuktu Pro for Networks. A new program that combines remote control and remote node technology in one package for both Windows and Macintosh users. Developed in conjunction with Shiva.

➡ *ISDN and the Future of Remote Access*

ISDN, which stands for Integrated Services Digital Network, is already beginning to have a great impact on remote access technology. ISDN carries voice, data, and video over digital circuits. This differs from traditional telephone lines which use analog transmission. Digital technology is faster and more accurate than its analog counterpart. How much faster? With ISDN you can transmit at 128Kbps. When you compare this to a speed that you are used to, such as 14.4 Kbps, you can see how fast ISDN really is and the implications it can have on processing large amounts of data. ISDN availability is expanding rapidly throughout the United States, with providers such as Pacific Bell, GTE, US West, and Southwestern Bell offering ISDN services.

ISDN also is making other new technologies faster and more feasible than ever before. An example is the concept of production telecommuting. Production telecommuting makes image-based applications available at remote sites. Using electronic workflow technology combined with the speed ISDN offers, remote workers can access document images as quickly as their office-based counterparts. One sample product is Unisys's InfoImage Folder, which uses this technology to process insurance claims, applications, and other records.

Contact Information

Manufacturer	Address	Phone
Farallon Computing	2470 Mariner Square Loop Alameda, CA 94501-1010	510-814-5000
LinkPro	4029 Westerly Place #201B Newport Beach, CA 92660	714-833-3322
Microcom	500 River Ridge Drive Norwood, MA 02062-5028	800-822-8224
Norton-Lambert	P.O. Box 4085 Santa Barbara, CA 93140	805-964-6767

Contact Information (Continued)

Manufacturer	Address	Phone
Shiva	Northwest Park 63 Third Avenue Burlington, MA 01803	800-977-4482
Stac	12636 High Bluff Drive San Diego, CA 92130-2093	800-677-6232
Symantec	10201 Torre Avenue Cupertino, CA 95014-2132	800-441-7234
Telebit	One Executive Drive Chelmsford, MA 01824	800-989-8888
Traveling Software	18702 North Creek Parkway Bothell, WA 98011	800-343-8080
Triton Technologies	200 Middlesex Turnpike Iselin, NJ 08830	800-322-9440
Unisys	P.O. Box 500 Blue Bell, PA 19424-0001	800-448-1424

6

Online *Services* and the *Telecommuter*

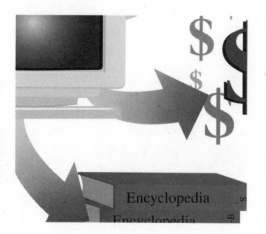

As a telecommuter, you won't have access to the company resources, information, and personnel that your office-based associates have. Through online information services, however, your computer can bring the news and information you need directly to you, rivaling any corporate reference center. And if you're missing the workplace camaraderie, online forums devoted to other home-based and mobile workers can provide a virtual community of like-minded people.

Most of the major online services include the following basic features:

- E-mail with connections to other online services and the Internet
- Forums covering special interests including technical, business, professional, and lifestyle topics with message and file download areas
- Reference materials and databases
- News, weather, and sports
- Travel information and resources
- Entertainment news and reviews
- Stock quotes and financial information
- Access to the Internet (including newsgroups, ftp, and the World Wide Web)

The variety and depth of coverage in each area varies from service to service, as each has particular strengths and weaknesses. Prices also vary, and you can often find the identical information or database on different services at different prices. As a telecommuter, your primary reasons for using an online service will probably be to exchange e-mail and documents, use online research and reference materials, and possibly communicate with other home-based workers. Here's an overview of the best-known online services and what they have to offer.

Connecting to CompuServe

CompuServe currently has 2.7 million users around the world. Of all the large on-line services, it offers the widest variety of forums on business and technical topics with the most in-depth coverage, as well as the greatest access to international resources and users. In March 1995 CompuServe acquired SPRY, maker of the Internet access software Internet In A Box and Mosaic In A Box. This acquisition is anticipated to greatly expand CompuServe's Internet offering by mid-1995.

CompuServe's pricing strategy groups its services into three main categories—basic (free under the Standard Pricing Plan), extended (hourly), and premium (hourly plus varying surcharges).

Basic Services Includes the following services for Standard Pricing Plan members:

 Basic stock quotes and company overviews

 CompuServe Mail (per-message charges apply after $9 worth of usage)

 EAASY SABRE and WORLDSPAN Travelshopper online travel reservations services

 Money Magazine's FundWatch Online mutual fund database

More than 30 syndicated columns on health, lifestyle, entertainment, finance, home, and family

News from a variety of sources around the world

Online versions of the *American Heritage Dictionary*, *Consumer Reports*, *Grolier's Academic American Encyclopedia*, and *Peterson's College Database*, as well as other reference resources

Restaurant, hotel, and sightseeing reviews

Extended and Premium Services Includes the following sources:

News. Includes news and weather reports from around the world, AP, Reuters, and a searchable news database, Newsgrid.

Computers. Offers technical support forums for more than 500 software and hardware companies as well as general-interest computer forums on IBM-compatible, Macintosh, Amiga, and other computer platforms.

Reference. Offers an extensive reference library. You can find the *American Heritage Dictionary*, numerous searchable business and technical databases, a legal research center, census information, a who's who directory, encyclopedia, demographic information, patent and trademark research, and a medical library all in this section.

➜ Professional. Provides forums and databases geared toward a variety of professionals such as broadcast engineers, court reporters, computer trainers, entrepreneurs, home-based workers, journalists, lawyers, and medical practitioners.

➜ Finance. Offers a wide variety of financial resources including international company profiles, stock and mutual fund quotes, online investing, and detailed investment analyses. Offerings include Commodity Markets, D&B Dun's Market Identifiers, European Company Library, Pricing History, S&P Online, and TRW Business Profiles.

➜ Travel. Includes access to American Airlines EAASY SABRE, the OAG Electronic Edition, Department of State advisories, as well as general-interest and country-specific travel forums.

~🖥~

CompuServe offers two pricing plans. The *Standard pricing plan* costs $9.95 per month and offers unlimited access to all basic services. It also povides a connect-time rate of $4.80 per hour for extended and premium services for access up to 14.4 Kbps, and $9 per month credit toward CompuServe Mail (approximately 90 three-page full-text messages).

The Standard plan provides free access to Executive Services option, offering the following:

➜ Access to numerous financial and business databases
➜ Volume discounts for use of selected financial databases
➜ Storage in Personal File Area for six months
➜ Ten percent discount on CompuServe products
➜ Fifty percent increase in storage capacity in Personal File Area

The *Alternative pricing plan* starts with a membership support fee of $2.50 per month. For the rest, it's pay-as-you-go. Connect-time is billed for all services (including CompuServe Mail) at the following rates: $6.30 per hour (300 bps),

$12.80 per hour (1,200 or 2,400 bps), and $22.80 per hour (9,600 and 14,400 bps).

Unless you are planning to use CompuServe very infrequently, for example only to access a specific database once a month, you will save a lot by joining the Standard pricing plan. Connect-time adds up quickly, particularly when you are "browsing" with a high-speed modem.

You can access CompuServe through any of the communications programs reviewed in Chapter 4, many of which contain special scripts for logging on to this service. You can also download special interface programs directly from the service such as the CompuServe Information Manager (GO CIMSOFT), which is available for DOS, Windows, OS2, and Macintosh. Other independent access programs also exist, such as OzCIS and TapCIS, which also help automate and reduce the cost of your online sessions. These are available in the OzCIS (GO OZCIS) and TapCIS (GO TAPCIS) forums.

Connecting to America Online

America Online is a general interest online service with about 2 million members in the United States. It is currently expanding internationally. America Online has a simple fee structure: $9.95 a month for the first five hours; $2.95 per hour after that. Highlights include

 Today's News. Offers details of the day's top general news stories as well as business, world, entertainment, sports, and weather news.

 Newsstand. Includes more than 60 online magazines such as *Business Week, Consumer Reports, Crain's Small Business, Home Office Computing, Investor's Business Daily, MacTech, Mobile Office, Newsbytes, PC World, Time, Windows,* and *Worth.*

 Personal Finance. Provides financial news and forums, stock quotes and portfolios as well as reference resources on mutual funds, stocks, taxes, and real estate. Also has a Small Business Center.

- Computing. Offers forums on a variety of computer topics: Hardware, Windows, Macintosh, Multimedia, Telecom & Networking, and DOS. Also has a Software Center with numerous files available to download.

- Travel. Provides access to American Airlines EAASY SABRE and several travel forums.

- Internet Connection. Includes ftp, newsgroups, Gopher & WAIS databases, and mailing lists.

Connecting to Prodigy

Prodigy charges $9.95 for up to five hours of usage per month, with additional hours charged at $2.95 each. It was the first major online service to release a Web Browser and currently has more than 450,000 of its members enrolled to use the browser. Specific offerings include

- News/Weather. Offers Quick News featuring Quick Business news clips; a Newsstand with online versions of *Consumer Reports*, *Newsweek*, *Newsday*, and *Kiplinger's*; weather reports from around the world, and access to AP Online.

- Business/Finance. Includes business news, stock quotes, online trading, online banking, business bulletin boards, investment information (company reports, analysis of mutual funds and stocks) as well as Prodigy for Business, a Plus (surcharged) service. Prodigy for Business features the following:

  - D&B Solutions with access to Dun & Bradstreet databases
  - Small Business Advisor with business articles from LEXIS-NEXIS databases
  - The Filing Cabinet, offering business opportunity reports and more than 550 business and legal forms from McGraw Hill
  - HeadsUp, a personalized daily news clipping service
  - International Franchise Association franchise information

Reference. Features the *Academic American Encyclopedia* and *Home Office Computing's Software Guide*.

 Computers. Includes news and bulletin boards on a variety of computer software and hardware, product support from major vendors, and access to the ZiffNet service.

 Travel. Provides EAASY SABRE online travel reservation system from American Airlines, city guides to most major U.S. cities, as well as Fodor's Worldview service.

 Communications. Includes complete Internet access—e-mail, news-groups, ftp/gopher, and a World Wide Web browser.

Connecting to GEnie

GEnie, another general interest online service, charges $8.95 per month for up to four hours of connect-time with additional time charged at $3 per hour. The prime time surcharge is $9.50 per hour. In addition to its regular offerings, GEnie also offers premium services charged at varying rates above the standard connect rate. These include Charles Schwab Brokerage Services, Dow Jones News/Retrieval, GE Mail to Fax, the Official Airline Guides Electronic Edition Travel Service, QuikNews clipping service, Investment ANALY$T(SM), and other database research services.

GEnie's main strength for telecommuters is in its reference resources. Its Home Office Small Business RoundTable should also be of interest. Some areas to explore:

 Computing Services. Offers many RoundTables (forums) with message bulletin boards, files to download, and frequent RTCs (real-time conferences). RoundTables include Macintosh, IBM PC, Internet, Multimedia, Microsoft, Windows, BBS & Telecommunications, and Datacommunications RoundTables. Also provides a PC Catalog for computer comparison shopping and a fee-based computer news center.

 Travel Services. Includes the OAG Electronic Edition, American Airlines EAASY SABRE, as well as several travel-related RoundTables.

➡ Personal Finance & Investing. Offers Dow Jones News/Retrieval, Charles Schwab Brokerage Services, D&B Company Profiles, as well as stock quotes and other financial information services.

➡ News. Provides access to several Reuters newswires; a full-text version of Newsbytes, and electronic editions of *USA Today*, the *San Francisco Chronicle*, *Los Angeles Times*, *Boston Globe*, *Chicago Tribune*, and *Washington Post*.

➡ Career & Professional Services. Provides a meeting place/information center for professionals in the fields of medicine, law, education, business, and the arts. Also offers WorkPlace and Home Office Small Business RoundTables.

➡ Research & Reference Services. Includes access to DIALOG, Dun & Bradstreet, Dow Jones News/Retrieval, and powerful full-search reference databases (discussed in detail in Chapter 10). Reference resources include complete databases on patents, trademarks, and trade names as well as law, medicine, and business.

Connecting to Other Online Services

You may also want to look into some of the latest offerings in online services:

➡ **eWorld.** eWorld, from Apple Computer, debuted in 1994. It is currently available only for Macintosh users, but Windows software should be released soon. eWorld is priced at $8.95 per month for up to four hours, with subsequent hours charged at $2.95 each. eWorld is particularly strong in the area of Apple product support and also offers technical support on other computer products, up-to-the-minute news, online travel planning, stock quotes, and financial information.

➡ **Interchange.** Developed by Ziff-Davis Interactive and recently acquired by AT&T, Interchange is particularly strong in the areas of computer information and support. It contains text from Ziff-Davis publications including *PC Magazine*, *PC Week*, *PC/Computing*, *Computer Shopper*, and *Windows Sources*, as well as reference, business, entertainment, and news resources. Interchange supports multi-tasking (for example, you can download a file and read mail at the same time) and will be available commercially in mid-1995.

➡ **The Microsoft Network (MSN).** Microsoft Network will be instantly available to all modem-equipped Windows 95 users when that product is released, most likely in August 1995. In addition to the traditional on-line service offerings such as business, lifestyle, education, reference, and entertainment information, MSN will be particularly strong in providing technical support and information on Microsoft products.

How to Contact Online Services

Service	Telephone
America Online	800-827-6364
CompuServe	800-848-8199
eWorld	800-775-4556
GEnie	800-638-9636
Interchange	800-595-8555
Microsoft Network	800-426-9400
Prodigy	800-776-3449

Connecting to the Internet

Everyone is talking about the Information Superhighway lately, and the Internet is an integral part of this. Started in 1969 as an experiment by the Department of Defense, and once primarily populated by government and academic users, the Internet today is a vast web of networks serving millions of users around the world.

What does the Internet have to offer? In some ways it's like an online service with information on business, computer technology, travel, shopping, finance, education, and entertainment. But the Internet is unregulated, with content provided by thousands of diverse groups, individuals, and organizations. Finding information on the Internet used to be a monumental task, but now that many "friendly" graphical user interfaces have been developed, navigating the Internet has become much easier and more productive than it was in the past. The Internet offers a variety of ways to access its rich resources. Here are some of the most common:

➡ **Electronic mail**   You can send e-mail to users around the world via the Internet, including those on various online services such as Compu-Serve, America Online, GEnie, Prodigy, and MCI Mail.

➡ **Ftp**   Ftp stands for file transfer protocol and offers a way for you to download files from a remote host computer.

➡ **Mailing lists**   Internet mailing lists are subject-specific e-mail exchanges. To participate you must subscribe to the mailing list (by sending an e-mail to the defined e-mail mailing list address) and unsubscribe to stop receiving mail from the list.

➡ **Newsgroups**   Newsgroups are message boards where users can post information about or discuss a specific topic.

➡ **Telnet**   Using Telnet you can access remote computers and their files and data.

➡ **World Wide Web**   Commonly known as the Web or WWW, the World Wide Web is a graphical Internet browser using hypertext links and complex graphics. The Web is currently the Internet "hot spot" and hundreds of new Web sites are being created every day.

Many computer users will connect to the Internet via an online service such as CompuServe or Prodigy, but you can also get an account with an Internet provider and use special access software to reach the Internet. Windows 95 will also have the option to directly connect to the Internet and will offer several basic Internet utilities, but you will still probably want to use a third-party tool for browsing the Internet, and particularly the Web. The following programs offer a graphical user interface to access the Internet and automatic signup with a variety of Internet providers:

 Spry Internet In A Box ($149) or Mosaic In A Box ($49.95), a Web browser. 800-777-9638

 NetManage Internet Chameleon ($199). 408-973-7171

➡ *Where Telecommuters Congregate Online*

Whether you are looking for resources or just want to chat with other home-based workers/telecommuters, the following online forums offer message boards, conferences, and libraries full of informational files and software suited to your needs.

➡ CompuServe's Working from Home Forum (GO WORK)

➡ GEnie's Home Office/Small Business RoundTable (HOSB)

➡ GEnie's WorkPlace RoundTable (WORKPLACE)

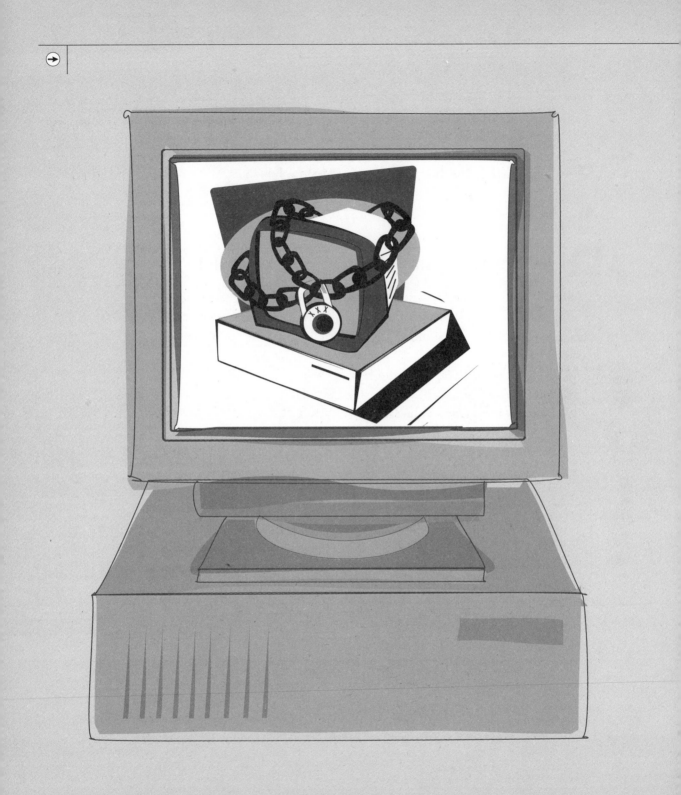

7 Telecommuting Computer Security Issues

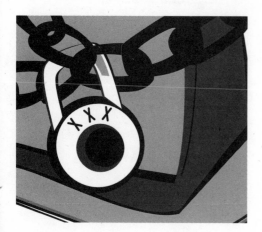

As a remote computer user, you are exposed to more data security risks than your office-based counterparts. The specters of computer viruses and stolen passwords and data access cards should point toward learning more about protecting your data. This chapter discusses how you can protect your data from viruses and unauthorized access.

Protecting Your Data from Computer Viruses

Michelangelo. Jerusalem-B. Black Monday. Dark Avenger. These names have made headlines in recent years regarding their destructive effects on computer systems around the world. In addition to these highly publicized viruses, there are at least 2,000 more, each of which can cause inconvenience or destruction on your computer system.

A virus is basically a computer program that attaches itself to another program and replicates, allowing itself to be spread from computer to computer via disk or network. It can merely slow down or interrupt your system, or it can destroy data. Similar to viruses, and potentially as destructive, are trojan horses, logic bombs, and worms.

In most cases, it will be apparent that your computer has a virus, but subtle viruses may be more difficult to detect, which is why establishing a virus detection system for your computer is essential.

Computer viruses can be spread in a number of ways:

- ➡ By exchanging disks
- ➡ By downloading files through a modem
- ➡ Via a network

Although computer viruses are usually created with malicious intent, they are often spread unknowingly by computer users who aren't aware that their data is infected. As a result, a computer virus can spread throughout the world, jumping from one computer system or network to another.

As a person involved in either telecommuting or mobile computing, your risk of having data infected by a computer virus will increase over those who work at a single workstation.

To lessen the chance of your data falling prey to virus infection you should

→ Educate yourself about computer viruses and how they are spread (Industrial Video Production's 23-minute video *The Computer Virus and How to Control It* is a great introduction).

→ Use antivirus software.

→ Back up your data regularly.

→ Refuse to share software with other users (in the case of commercial software, this is also illegal).

Many people who frequently use computers have had their data infected by a virus at one time or another. Even computer professionals, who are educated in the detection of viruses, will get their data infected at times. My one and only experience with a computer virus occurred when a co-worker asked for my assistance in printing a file, and before I could stop him, he had inserted his disk into my floppy drive and turned on my computer. The disk was infected with a virus and soon, so was my computer.

Suggested Programs

Users of DOS versions 6 and above have basic virus protection through the MSAV command. You might also want to consider using a third-party virus detector, however. Many shareware virus detectors currently exist, which you can download from the online service areas listed below. Some good commercial software choices include

Reflex Disknet 2.15

→ Prevents the use of floppy disks that have not been certified virus-free

→ Automatically cures partition/boot sector viruses

→ Especially suitable for networks

→ Keeps pirated and unauthorized software off company networks

→ Retail price: $135

→ *Understanding Software Licensing*

Using unauthorized copies of software isn't only illegal, it can also increase the possibility of spreading computer viruses as well as prevent you from getting vendor technical support. Telecommuting and mobile computing open the door for many complications in the area of software licensing, particularly in a certain gray area concerning individual users who work with more than one computer system.

Individual licensing is very straightforward if you have only one computer and purchase software only for that system. But what if you have two computer systems, but never use them at the same time, such as both an office and a home computer or both a desktop and notebook system? According to the document *Understanding Licensing Agreements,* published by the Software Publishers Association, certain interpretations of individual licensing "...may include the single user being allowed, under the terms of the license, to make a copy of the software for his/her home PC and/or laptop computer. The idea here is that the user cannot be in more than one place at a time. Therefore, the software can only be used in one place at a time."

Does this mean you can routinely load one copy of a software program on all computer systems you use? Not necessarily, as it depends on each company's interpretation of software licensing. If in doubt, contact the vendor's customer support line to verify.

Symantec AntiVirus for Macintosh (SAM) 4.0

- ➔ Includes Power Macintosh version of Virus Clinic for faster virus scanning
- ➔ Updates the virus definitions file via modem
- ➔ Scans compressed disks
- ➔ Allows creation of decontamination disks
- ➔ Retail price: $99

Symantec Norton AntiVirus 3.0 (Windows)

➡ Detects 100 percent of known viruses in the NCSA library

➡ Offers ability to detect unknown viruses via the Symantec-NOVI Virus Sensor Technology

➡ Is able to scan files compressed with PKZIP

➡ Includes sophisticated password protection

➡ Retail price: $129

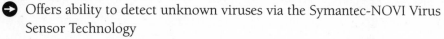

For more information, check the following sources.

The Internet

➡ VIRUS-L FAQ (frequently asked questions). Anonymous ftp to cert.org in the file pub/virus-l/FAQ.virus.l

➡ VIRUS-L mailing list. Subscribe by sending the message "SUB VIRUS-L JOHN SMITH" (substituting your own name) to LISTSERV@ LEHIGH.EDU.

➡ Comp.virus USENET newsgroup

CompuServe

➡ Symantec AntiVirus Forum (GO SYMVIR)

➡ National Computer Security Association Forum (GO NCSA), which includes the NCSA Virus Vendor Forum and the NCSA InfoSecurity Forum

➡ KAOS AntiVirus Forum (GO ANTIVIRUS)

➡ McAfee Virus Forum (GO VIRUSFORUM)

➡ Cheyenne Software Forum (GO CHEYENNE)

➡ Michelangelo AntiVirus Area (GO MICHELANGELO)

America Online

➡ Virus Information Center (Keyword: Virus)

➡ McAfee Associates (Keyword: McAfee)

Data Security Issues

You also need to be concerned about remote access security. (Chapter 5 covers remote access technology and highlighted the built-in security features of a number of suggested programs.)

Why is security so important to remote access users? Computer hackers and their crimes have been making headlines with alarming frequency in the past few years. Hackers can access remote computers and steal or damage your data or even stop your system from operating. The old hacker stereotype of a young computer whiz involved in hacking as a way to prove technical competence is being replaced with a new hacker profile—that of a technologically sophisticated white-collar criminal, hacking for enormous potential profits.

As computer crimes continue to rise, employees participating in telecommuting and mobile computing need to be aware of the increased risks their flexible workstyle creates. According to Jan Masters of LeeMah DataCom Security Corporation, a manufacturer of remote access security systems, telecommuting and mobile computing present different security risks:

Telecommuting

 Often involves older technology that doesn't work with new remote access security systems (such as those that work with PCMCIA cards)

 Provides a more secure physical environment

Mobile Computing

 Offers even greater risks than telecommuting

 Increases the threat of "shoulder surfing" in which someone sitting or standing nearby could potentially watch you dial a number and enter your access code and password

Although selecting and implementing a remote access security system is usually within the realm of the Information Systems Department, as a remote access end user you need to understand the basic concepts of security.

Ted Phillips, Senior Associate with the McLean, Virginia-based consulting firm Booz.Allen & Hamilton, and a specialist in telecommunications system security, offers these suggestions:

- Don't allow direct access to any computer system without incorporating security measures (passwords, callback, encryption, authentication).

- Learn and use the existing security features of any equipment or software that you purchase.

- Maintain strict control of all proprietary information, including user names, passwords, printed or electronic company phone books, and old manuals and documentation.

- Don't give out any information over the phone to anyone claiming to be an employee without authentication.

- Perform regular security audits to make sure that your security systems are working.

- Establish security awareness in your company to train employees on security issues.

- Most important, develop a corporate security policy, endorsed and enforced by senior management, before implementing any remote access systems.

Are You Protecting Your Passwords?

Even though passwords alone don't comprise a complete security system today, many people make it even easier for potential intruders to access their systems by not properly safeguarding their passwords. According to *Security and Remote Access Computing: a Primer*, published by LeeMah DataCom Security Corporation, users frequently compromise the secrecy of their passwords in the following ways:

- Choosing obvious passwords, such as Social Security numbers or middle names, because they are easy to remember—but they are also easy to guess

➔ *Are You Protecting Your Passwords?*

➔ Writing down passwords that are difficult to remember and sticking them to their computer screens (or jotting them down in a notebook or organizer), making them easy to steal

➔ Programming passwords into dial strings of their communications software to automate the log-on process—and the hacking process as well

Data Security Systems

Contact the following companies to discuss their options for your data security needs.

Company	Address	Telephone
LeeMah DataCom Security Corporation	3948 Trust Way Hayward, CA 94545	800-824-9369 (within California) 800-992-0020 (outside of California)
Symantec Corporation	10201 Torre Avenue Cupertino, CA 95014-2132	800-441-7234
JCS and Associates (distributor for Reflex and Industrial Video Productions)	5025 Venture Drive Ann Arbor, MI 48108	800-968-9JCS

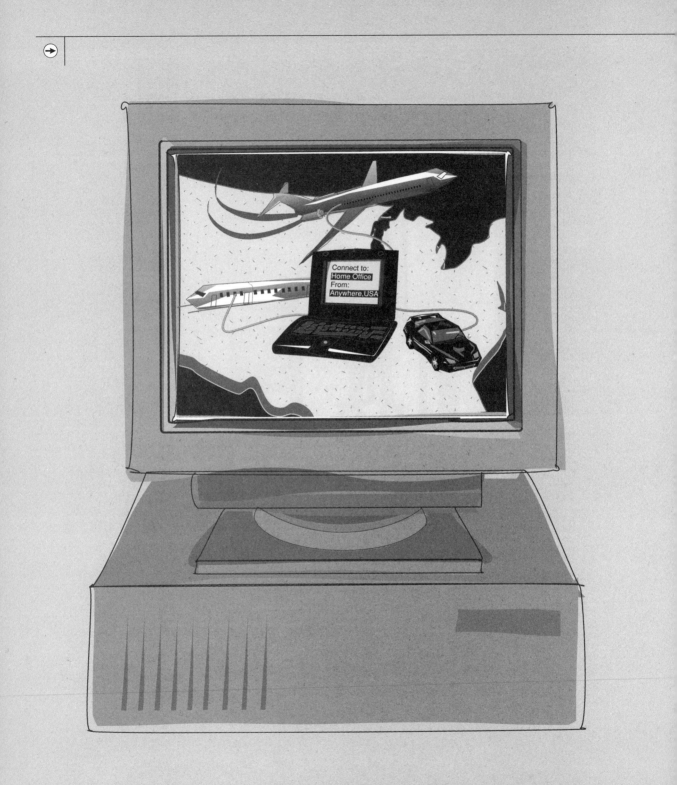

8 Technical Support from a Distance

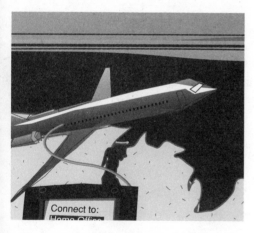

When

you're 200 miles from the office and your computer doesn't work, you need to be resourceful. Working away from the office can mean flexibility and freedom, but it can also mean that you have more responsibility to resolve computer problems than if you were in an office. The first step toward independence as a telecommuter is educating yourself on your computer system and software. Here are some suggestions:

- ➡ Develop a strong knowledge of the main programs you will be using.
- ➡ Build a library of computer reference materials to use when you have a problem.
- ➡ Learn to use system utility programs to diagnose and resolve many of your own computer problems.

Getting Computer Training

Although many software user manuals are very well written, some people find using a book a frustrating way to learn. Besides learning the program on your own through trial and error, what are your options?

Community Colleges/University Extensions/Adult Education Centers   These are your best bargains in computer education, however, there are some pitfalls. Classes often fill up quickly, the school may not have the latest technology, or you may have to wait a long time before an actual class begins. If you can get into a class and your local colleges have modern facilities, however, this is an excellent option.

Video Training   If you prefer a visual learning experience, video training is a good choice. Two suggestions:

- ➡ MacAcademy provides excellent videos on most Macintosh programs and also offers Mac training seminars throughout the country. Most videos are priced at $49.

➡ ViaGrafix specializes in Windows/DOS software videos. Their catalog includes over 280 videos on today's most popular applications as well as special video series on networking, CAD, programming, and Macintosh applications. Videos include an accompanying learning disk and range from $40 to $100 each.

~💻~

Computer-based Training   Computer-based training offers several advantages—you get hours of hands-on instruction, can work at your own pace, and can use the program to brush up on your skills months after initial training.

➡ *Allegro New Media*   Offers the following interactive CD-ROMs—Learn To Do Spreadsheets, Learn To Do Word Processing, Learn To Do Desktop Publishing, and Learn To Do Windows 3.1. These CD-ROMs include dozens of interactive lessons, the full-text of several reference books on each subject, and complete search capabilities. Retail prices range from $40 to $60.

➡ *InfoSource*   Provides Seminar-On-A-Disk training programs on floppy disk, and Seminar-On-A-Disc Multimedia Edition, programs on CD-ROM. CD versions include Windows, Word, Excel, and PowerPoint instruction. The disk version adds Lotus, Quattro Pro, WordPerfect, Paradox, Internet, and many other programs. Retail prices range from $160 for Seminar-On-A-Disk to $250 for Seminar-On-A-Disc Multimedia version.

➡ *ViaGrafix*   Produces several of its videos in a computer-based format, including Windows, Word, Access, PowerPoint, and Excel. Each is fully interactive with video and audio clips and retails for $50.

~💻~

Independent Computer Training Centers   Most independent training centers, particularly those that are vendor-authorized training facilities, provide quality hands-on training in a comfortable environment. You don't need to deal with the registration woes of signing up for college classes, don't have to wait for a semester to start, or go to class one night a week for months, but this convenience comes at a price. Independent training is your most expensive option. Before

➡ *Allegro's Learn To Do Word Processing*

```
┌─────────────────────────────────────────────────────────────┐
│ ─          Learn To Do Word Processing - Word            ▼ ▲ │
├─────────────────────────────────────────────────────────────┤
│ ┌───────┐                                                     │
│ │Section│  Formatting Documents                               │
│ │Contents│                                                    │
│ └───────┘                                                     │
│  [Show]  About Appearance ─────────────────────────      ✍   │
│  [Show]  Enhancing Text Appearance ──────────────  [Try] ✍   │
│  [Show]  Inserting Symbols & Special Characters ──  [Try] ✍   │
│  [Show]  Aligning Paragraphs ────────────────────  [Try] ✍   │
│  [Show]  Setting Tabs ───────────────────────────  [Try] ✍   │
│  [Show]  Setting Margins ────────────────────────  [Try] ✍   │
│  [Show]  Setting Indents ────────────────────────  [Try] ✍   │
│  [Show]  Controlling Page Breaks ────────────────  [Try] ✍   │
│  [Show]  Shading And Bordering Paragraphs ───────  [Try] ✍   │
│  [Show]  Creating Headers And Footers ───────────  [Try] ✍   │
│  [Show]  Displaying Different Views ──────────────  [Try] ✍   │
├─────────────────────────────────────────────────────────────┤
│  File   Contents  Back   Prev  Next  Notes  Search  Help      │
│                  History            < + >                     │
│                                              94.23%           │
└─────────────────────────────────────────────────────────────┘
```

signing up, verify that the training center provides one computer per student, that the facility is equipped with the latest technology, including the latest version of the software you want to learn, and that the course covers the topics you need most.

Two companies that offer excellent computer training at locations throughout the United States are New Horizons and ExecuTrain. Both organizations offer a wide variety of PC and Macintosh courses, provide discounts through the purchase of training coupons and computer clubs, and include after-class telephone support for class participants.

→ *Refining Your Skills*

Once you have mastered the basics of a software program, refining your skills, learning easy tricks and techniques, and finding solutions to sticky problems become more important. A local user group can help fill in these gaps. Although user groups don't normally offer basic instruction, they can be a great help once you know the fundamentals of a system or program. Most offer regular meetings with guest speakers and presentations on related topics, which provide a way for you to both stay current on the software you use most as well as to connect with other users. In most metropolitan areas there are dozens of user groups on topics ranging from generic PC or Macintosh use to specific software or specialties such as computer graphics, Visual Basic programming, desktop publishing, or online communications. You can find out about user groups in your area through listings in local computer publications or through local computer dealers.

Using System Utility Software

To ensure that your system is running at optimal levels and that you have adequate protection in case of disaster, you should purchase and install system utility software on your computer.

What can system utility software do for you?

- → Diagnose and repair system problems
- → Restore deleted files
- → Prevent system crashes
- → Scan for viruses
- → Unformat hard or floppy disks
- → Automatically repair corrupted data
- → Encrypt confidential files
- → Defragment your hard drive
- → Back up your data

Symantec and Central Point Software, acquired by Symantec in 1994, produce some of the best system utility software on the market. Their products include:

- Mac Tools Pro 4.0
- Norton Utilities for Macintosh 3.0
- Norton Utilities for Windows 8.0
- PC Tools for Windows 2.0

Note that the Windows products will not function completely under Windows 95. Norton Utilities for Windows 95 will be the replacement product once Windows 95 is released.

Working with Your Company's Help Desk

If you work for a company that has a Help Desk to support its internal computer users, this should be your first stop if you can't resolve a problem yourself. Let the Help Desk staff know that you are working from home or a mobile office so that they will already be prepared to handle your requests when you call. Using remote access software, such as pcANYWHERE, Laplink, or Carbon Copy, described in Chapter 5, a Help Desk representative can control your computer system in order to diagnose and resolve problems while visually demonstrating the solutions to you.

Getting Vendor Technical Support

If you can't fix a problem yourself, and your company Help Desk isn't available, or if you don't have a Help Desk, contacting the software vendor's technical support staff will be the next step to take. There are three main ways to contact a vendor about its product:

 Telephone Support   Almost all computer software and hardware companies provide telephone support on their products. Some provide this support for free, through a toll-free number, and offer extended service hours. Others charge for support or only provide it during regular working hours. If you want a fast response to your question, this should be your first choice, assuming the support center is open and is free to you.

 Fax-on-Demand   If you have a fax machine at home, or can receive faxes through your computer, fax-on-demand can be a convenient solution. Vendor fax-on-demand systems allow you to order specific technical support documents by phone and receive them by fax, almost instantly. Your first call to the fax-on-demand system will usually be to request a list of available documents. After that you can order whatever you need by its document number. Since this system is automated, it's also available 24 hours a day, at your convenience. The main disadvantage is that fax-on-demand is only useful if the information you need is included in their document list.

 Online Services   As the number of computer users with online access climbs into the millions, more computer companies are providing online technical support for their users. Online support comes in several forms—company-sponsored BBSs, information via the Internet (particularly company Web sites), and technical support forums on commercial online services such as CompuServe, America Online, Prodigy, and eWorld.

CompuServe, in particular, offers extensive technical support from more than 500 hardware and software companies. Each of these vendor forums includes libraries of product and technical information, and you may be able to find an immediate answer in one of these files. Particularly noteworthy are the following:

- Apple Technical Information Library includes more than 4,500 articles on Apple products. Entering **GO APLTIL** will access this library.

- Lotus Technical Library provides more than 8,000 files on Lotus products. To access, type **GO LTL**.

- Microsoft's KnowledgeBase includes more than 35,000 documents on Microsoft documents and provides answers to many common user questions. To access, enter **GO MSKB**.

- ZiffNet's Support On Site includes more than 92,000 technical support documents from various Ziff sources. Typing **GO ONSITE** will access this area.

CompuServe's Technical Resources

You can use CompuServe to access libraries of technical information.

```
┌─────────────────────────────────────────────────────────────┐
│ ─                CompuServe Information Manager          ▼ ▲ │
├─────────────────────────────────────────────────────────────┤
│ File   Edit   Help                                           │
│ ┌──────────────────────────────────────────────────────────┐│
│ │?│ Connected    ┌─┐  ┌─┐  ┌─┐  ┌─┐  ┌────┐               ││
│ │ │    8:58      └─┘  └─┘  └─┘  └─┘  │EXIT│               ││
│ ├──────────────────────────────────────────────────────────┤│
│ │                    Support on Site                        ││
│ │      Found 67 product names                               ││
│ │  Select a product:                                        ││
│ │  ┌──────────────────────────────────────────────┬─────┬─┐ ││
│ │  │ lotus 1-2-3 for windows                 2229  │  ▲  │ ││
│ │  │ lotus 1-2-3/g                            308  │     │ ││
│ │  │ lotus ami pro                           1082  │     │ ││
│ │  │ lotus approach                           649  │     │ ││
│ │  │ lotus cc:mail                            157  │     │ ││
│ │  │ lotus freelance for dos                  831  │     │ ││
│ │  │ lotus freelance for os/2                 177  │     │ ││
│ │  │ lotus freelance for windows              551  │     │ ││
│ │  │ lotus improv                             199  │     │ ││
│ │  │ lotus notes                              108  │     │ ││
│ │  │ lotus organizer                          154  │     │ ││
│ │  │ lotus smartsuite for windows              11  │  ▼  │ ││
│ │  └──────────────────────────────────────────────┴─────┴─┘ ││
│ │        ┌──────────────┐      ┌──────────────┐             ││
│ │        │      OK      │      │    Cancel    │             ││
│ │        └──────────────┘      └──────────────┘             ││
│ └──────────────────────────────────────────────────────────┘│
└─────────────────────────────────────────────────────────────┘
```

And even if you don't find your answer in these extensive support libraries, you can leave a message in the forum bulletin board and will probably receive a reply from a company representative within 24 hours. Other users may also contribute useful replies to your request. CompuServe offers a support directory where you can keyword search a database of more than 1,000 items to find the right place to get support on a particular computer product. You can reach this directory by typing **GO SUPPORT**.

Other online services such as Prodigy, America Online, GEnie, and eWorld have similar online technical support, particularly for large computer companies, but none match the comprehensiveness of CompuServe.

Contact information for these online services is provided in Chapter 6. Information on the phone, fax, and online technical support that major vendors provide is included in Appendix B.

Building a Reference Library

Creating a strong reference library of books on the software you use most will save you hours trying to figure out how to perform specific tasks in that software. Ziff-Davis Press, the publisher of this book, has two excellent series that cover today's most popular software packages—the PC Learning Labs series and the How to Use series. If you're looking for a more visual reference, Allegro New Media offers a ready-made reference library—the Home PC Library CD-ROM. This CD offers the full-text of 21 computer books covering the following topics: modems, printers, DOS, Windows, CD-ROM, and online services and is fully searchable. Its retail price is $60.

Technical Support Resources

Manufacturer	Address	Phone
Allegro New Media	16 Passaic Avenue Fairfield, NJ 07004	800-424-1992
InfoSource	6947 University Boulevard Winter Park, FL 32792	800-393-4636
MacAcademy	477 South Nova Road Ormond Beach, FL 32174-8452	800-527-1914
Symantec Corporation	10201 Torre Avenue Cupertino, CA 95014	800-441-7234
ViaGrafix	5 S. Vann Street Pryor, OK 74361	800-842-4723

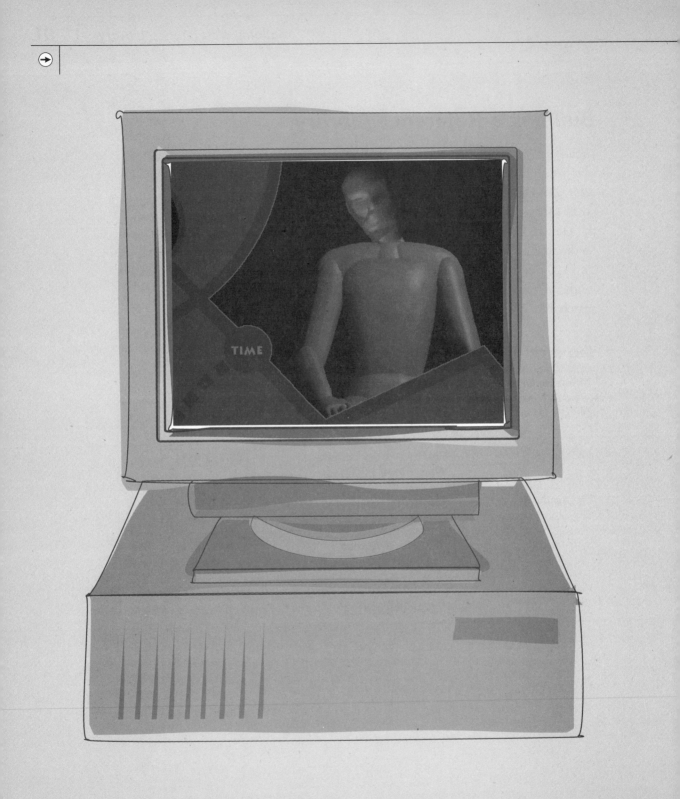

9 *Additional Software*

When you work from home or a mobile location, you often don't have access to the traditional information resources a regular office provides. In many cases, you also won't have the room to store extensive reference materials, particularly if your job involves travel.

The Best Software for the Remote Office

The following list of software titles represents a collection of my personal favorites that includes basic reference materials and business resources as well as a program to keep you healthy while working for long periods of time at your computer.

Allegro Business 500 (Windows)

 Offers histories, stock/financial details, and contact information for more than 500 U.S. companies

 Provides content from *Hoover's Handbook of American Business*

 Includes videos of company product presentations and executive speeches

 Allows downloads of company update information from the Prodigy online service

 Retail price: $50

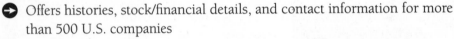

Allegro Business Library CD-ROM (Windows)

 Includes the full text of 12 business books: *Business to Business Communications Handbook, The Feel of Success in Selling, Finance & Accounting for Nonfinancial Managers, How to Get People to Do Things Your Way, How to Make Big Money in Real Estate in the Tighter, Tougher '90s Market, International Herald Tribune Guide to Business Travel EUROPE, Joyce Lain Kennedy's Career Book, Meetings Rules & Procedures, State of the Art Marketing Research, Successful Direct Marketing Methods, Successful Telemarketing,* and *Total Global Strategy: Managing for Worldwide Competitive Advantage*

➜ Provides three complete videos: *30 Timeless Direct Marketing Principles, From Advertising to Integrated Marketing Communications,* and *New Product Development*

➜ Offers powerful searching capabilities

➜ Provides hundreds of illustrations, tables, charts, and diagrams

➜ Retail price: $60

➜ **The table of contents for** How to Get People To Do Things Your Way**, included in Allegro Business Library.**

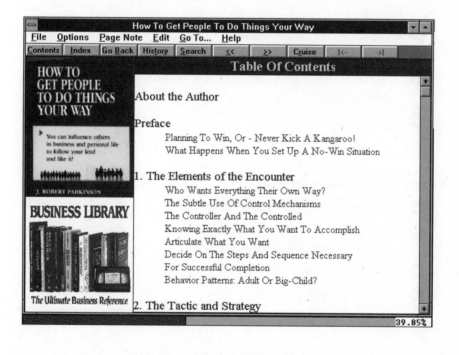

Compton's Interactive Encyclopedia 3.0 (Windows/Macintosh)

➜ Contains all 35,000 articles from the 26-volume print version of *Compton's Encyclopedia*

- Idea Search feature allows users to ask basic questions and receive answers
- Includes 15 hours of audio; over 8,000 images; more than 100 video clips; animations; maps; and charts
- Owners of previous version can upgrade for $49.95
- Retail price: $80

Digital Directory Assistance PhoneDisc PowerFinder (Windows/Macintosh)

- Fully searchable directory of 91 million business and residential phone listings
- Includes reverse indexing to find listings by address or phone number
- Exports to PIMS, databases, and contact managers
- Also offers residential-only and business-only directories without reverse indexing for $79
- Retail price: $249

Ergodyne WorkSmart Stretch (DOS)

- Includes 3D animation to guide users through stretching exercises
- Offers stretches for neck and shoulders, upper extremities, lower body, and back (the areas most affected by prolonged use of a computer)
- Reminds users to stretch every 50 minutes
- Retail price: $50

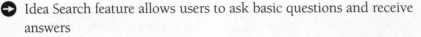

Globalink PowerTranslator (DOS/Windows/Macintosh)

- Translates words and documents from and to the foreign language
- Particularly useful for translating foreign language documents into basic English
- Includes more than 250,000 dictionary entries

***One of the exercises found in Ergodyne WorkSmart
Stretch***

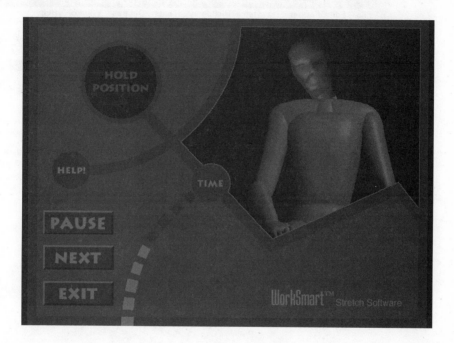

 Provides grammar reference tool

 Available in French, Spanish, and German

 Retail price: $149

Great Bear 401 Great Letters for Windows

 Includes 115 business letters, 115 customer letters, 115 office letters,
and 56 personal letters

 Knowledge Accelerator helps find the appropriate letter quickly

 Includes full word processing capabilities with option to export to external word processor

Globalink Power Translater Deluxe can translate basic business letters into a foreign language.

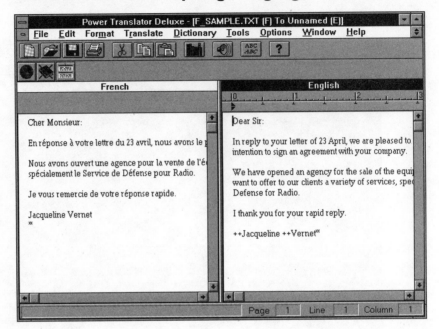

 Also offers *101 Sales & Marketing Letters* or *101 Professional Letters* for $40

 Retail price: $50

Grolier 1995 Multimedia Encyclopedia (Windows/Macintosh)

 Includes 33,000 articles from the *Academic American Encyclopedia*

 Offers 325 interactive maps, including 55 city maps

 Related concept searching assists in sophisticated topic searches

 Provides hours of sound clips, more than 8,000 photographs, and numerous illustrations

 Retail price: $150

Microsoft Bookshelf (Windows)

 Offers seven major reference works including *The American Heritage Dictionary, The Original Roget's Thesaurus, The Columbia Dictionary of Quotations, The Concise Columbia Encyclopedia,* and *Hammond Intermediate World Atlas.*

➔ Provides sound, video, and animation as well as 80,000 spoken pronunciations

➔ Retail price: $80

Random House Unabridged Electronic Dictionary 1.7 (Windows)

➔ Includes 315,000 entries

➔ Offers 115,000 recorded pronunciations and 2,200 graphics

➔ Provides ability to look up a word in any document

➔ Retail price: $79

Teneron LegalPoint 1.0 (Windows)

➔ Includes over 70 editable legal documents, many business related

➔ Offers online legal guidance, tips, and definitions

➔ Covers financial, marketing, sales, personnel, corporate, technology, real estate, and estate planning topics

➔ Retail price: $99

➡ *Finding Business Shareware*

You can find quality shareware in two ways: by purchasing a shareware CD-ROM or by downloading shareware from a BBS or online service. There are advantages to both methods. CD-ROMs provide a way to inexpensively try out hundreds of programs for only the cost of the CD. Downloading the same amount of shareware from an online service could become prohibitively expensive. But if you're looking for a specific kind of shareware, you will probably do better searching for it on an online service and downloading it, rather than trying to find a CD-ROM that has that particular program or one that performs a specific function.

Walnut Creek CDROM produces a good Windows shareware CD called CICA for Windows that includes utilities, demos of commercial products, screen savers, icons, fonts, tutorials, and technical information on popular software, as well as many application programs. Some examples of the more than 3,000 files are Time and Chaos, an appointment calendar/phone book, and WinZip, a Windows compression utility.

In the online world, ZiffNet offers a wide variety of shareware in its sections on online services such as CompuServe and Prodigy. A recent file search on ZiffNet via CompuServe found nearly 17,000 DOS/Windows files and almost 6,000 Macintosh entries including programs such as Business Letters (BUSLTR.ZIP) which includes 600 sample business letters, Understanding the Internet WinHelp file (UNDER.ZIP), and PkZip 2.04G (PK204G.EXE) which will allow you to decompress these zipped files. To access ZiffNet on CompuServe enter **GO ZIFFNET**; on Prodigy it's **JUMP: ZIFFNET**.

Where to Find the Best Software for the Remote Office

Manufacturers	Address	Phone
Allegro New Media	16 Passaic Avenue Fairfield, NJ 07004	800-424-1992
Compton NewMedia	2320 Camino Vida Roble Carlsbad, CA 92009-1504	800-284-2045
Digital Directory Assistance	6931 Arlington Road, Suite 405 Bethesda, MD 20814-5231	800-284-8353
Ergodyne	1410 Energy Park Drive, Suite 1 St. Paul, MN 55108	800-225-8238
Globalink	9302 Lee Highway Fairfax, VA 22031	800-255-5660
Great Bear Technology	1100 Moraga Way, Suite 200 Moraga, CA 94556	800-795-4325
Grolier Electronic Publishing	Sherman Turnpike Danbury, CT 06816	800-285-4534
Microsoft		800-426-9400
Random House Reference and Electronic Publishing	Third Floor 201 East 50th Street New York, NY 10022-7703	801-228-9933
Teneron Corporation	7300 West 110th Street, Suite 630 Overland Park, KS 66210	800-529-5669
Walnut Creek CDROM	4041 Pike Lane, Suite D-386 Concord, CA 94520	800-786-9907

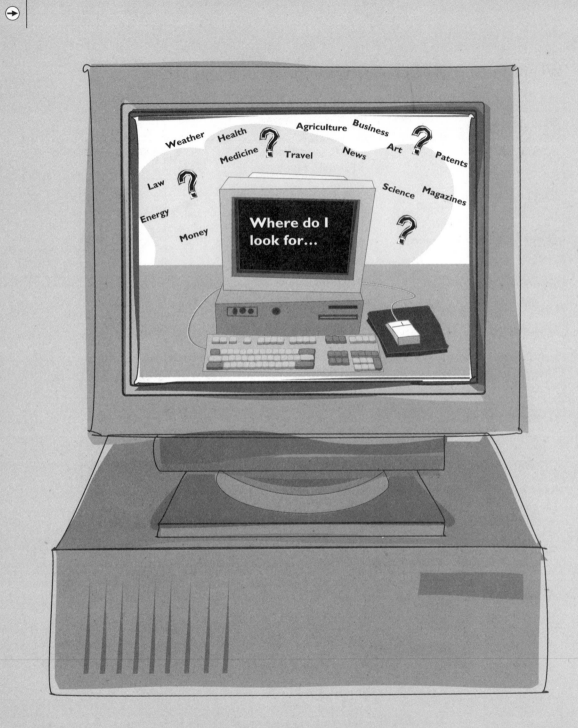

10 *Online Research*

As we enter the information age, more and more resources formerly available only in printed form now can be accessed by anyone with a computer and modem. Newspapers, magazines, trade journals, reference manuals, and research reports from around the world can all be searched online. Coverage is varied, but science, technology, business, law, and medicine are the most common topics of online databases. What exactly is an online database? Different terms mean different things to different people. As a result, the terms *online database* and *online service* are occasionally used interchangeably and are therefore confused with each other.

The term online service is generally used to describe general-interest online services like America Online, GEnie, and CompuServe, as discussed in Chapter 6. An online database, however, is highly specialized and contains detailed information on a specific topic. If you want to look up a subject in an encyclopedia or find reviews of software products, you can find this information in most any general-interest online service. If you want to gather details about recent mergers and acquisitions in the pharmaceutical industry or research Chinese legal proceedings, you will need to search a specialized online database.

A database provider is similar to a consumer online service like CompuServe or America Online in that you access it via a modem and follow a menu system or issue commands to reach the information you need. Some online services now offer a gateway to a database provider. For example, CompuServe offers a gateway to Knowledge Index and IQUEST, offering databases from providers such as DIALOG, DataStar, NewsNet, and Questel•Orbit. GEnie offers a gateway to Dow Jones News/Retrieval and DIALOG. All of the gateway services are surcharged.

This chapter will give you a brief overview of what's available where and how much it will cost. It's by no means comprehensive, but should give you an idea of where to start.

Research on Consumer Online Services

CompuServe and GEnie are the online services with the most comprehensive online research offerings. Other services, such as Prodigy and America Online, do

have some basic reference material, but theirs are not nearly as complete as CompuServe and GEnie's. One of these services may very well provide everything
that you need for research.

~⌨~

CompuServe   The following are the most comprehensive databases on
CompuServe:

➜ Knowledge Index (GO KI) offers evening and weekend access to more
than 100 popular online databases, including databases on agriculture,
the arts, science, technology, law, medicine, business, and engineering.
The complete text of many major newspapers such as the *Los Angeles
Times*, *Chicago Tribune*, and *Washington Post* are also included, as are two
major newswires. Because it is only available outside of normal business
hours, Knowledge Index charges $24 per hour, including CompuServe
connect charges, making it a good value for those whose schedules are
flexible enough to allow off-hours searching.

➜ IQuest (GO IQUEST) provides access to more than 800 databases from
information providers such as DIALOG, NewsNet, Questel•Orbit, and
DataStar, detailed below. IQuest is available 24 hours a day. Costs vary
depending on the database and are charged by the search, but in general,
IQuest is more expensive than Knowledge Index.

Here are some other samples of CompuServe's numerous reference resources:

➜ Business Database Plus (GO BUSDB) offers two collections of current
business information sources. Integrated Business and Trade Information
(called Business and Trade Journals if using terminal emulation) provides
business-related articles from the last five years from more than 750 business magazines, newspapers, and journals. Industry Newsletters offers
two years' worth of information from more than 500 business newsletters. Business Database Plus charges a $15 per hour surcharge in addi-
tion to regular CompuServe connect time.

➜ Computer Database Plus (GO COMPDB) covers all aspects of the computer industry, with articles from more than 230 publications including
Byte, *PC Magazine*, and *MacUser*. $15 surcharge per hour, in addition to
regular connect charges.

CompuServe's reference menu

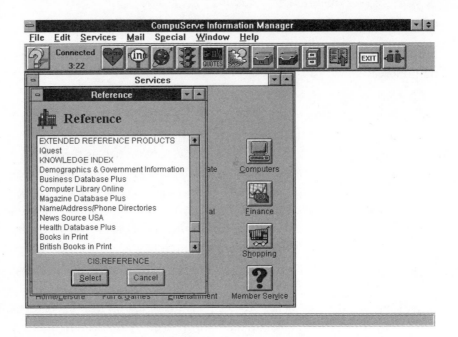

 Executive News Service (GO ENS) scans through UPI, AP, and Reuters for specified news topics. Surcharged at $15 per hour.

 International Company Information (GO COINTL) offers numerous databases with details on millions of companies around the world. Sample databases include: S&P Online, D&B Dun's Market Identifiers, Corporate Affiliations, TRW Business Credit Profile, European Company Research Centre, Telefirm: Directory of French Companies, BDI German Industry, German Company Research Center, British Trade Marks, ICC Directory of U.K. Companies, Australian/New Zealand Company Research Centre, and Hoppenstedt Benelux. Searches average $7.50 to $15.

 Legal Research Center (GO LEGALRC) offers two legal databases with articles from more than 750 law journals. Locating the appropriate database costs $1, retrieving 10 records is $5, as is retrieving one full-text record.

➡ Magazine Database Plus (GO MAGDB) includes general-interest articles from more than 130 popular magazines ranging from *Time* to *Kiplinger's Personal Finance* to *Cosmopolitan*. Each article download is priced at $1.50.

➡ Newsgrid (GO NEWSGRID). Offers keyword searching of recent news stories. Not surcharged.

➡ Official Airlines Guide Electronic Edition Travel Service (GO OAG) offers an online travel reservation service in addition to several databases covering information on destinations, countries, cruises, airports, weather, dining, lodging, currency, tours, and travel industry news. OAG is surcharged at $10 per hour for evening/weekend use and $28 per hour for weekday usage.

➡ PaperChase (GO PAPERCHASE) provides access to MEDLINE, a comprehensive library of more than 7 million references from 4,000 medical journals dating back to 1966. Produced by the National Library of Medicine, PaperChase is surcharged at $18 per hour for evening/weekend use and $24 per hour for weekday usage.

➡ Patent Research Center (GO PATENT) includes several international patent databases. Prices range from $5 to $15 per patent record, depending on the database.

➡ Trademarkscan (GO TRADEMARK) comprises two databases covering current and pending trademark registrations throughout the United States. This section is priced at $20 for each group of five records.

~🖥~

GEnie GEnie's two major reference offerings include the following:

➡ Dow Jones News/Retrieval (DOWJONES) offers more than 50 databases providing extensive coverage on business and finance. Sample offerings include Disclosure Database, Mutual Funds Performance Report, and Corporate Ownership Watch, as well as the full text of the *Wall Street*

Journal and *Barron's*. Most databases are priced at $1.50 per 1,000 characters, but several charge by the report.

➤ DIALOG Database Center (DIALOG) is a comprehensive reference resource offering more than 400 databases covering business, finance, law, medicine, and science as well as many newspapers, newswires, and newsletters. Databases are priced based on retrieval. Some examples: Kompass Europe ($7.50), Drug Information Fulltext ($6.00), Business Dateline ($7.50), and Insider Trading Monitor ($4.50).

➤ **The opening screen for GEnie's research and reference services**

Here are some other GEnie reference resources:

- Dun & Bradstreet Databases (D&B) include six databases with U.S. and international company profiles. Charges are $7.50 for the initial search, retrieving up to five companies, and $7.50 for a full company record.

- GEnie QuikNews (QUIKNEWS) is a news-clipping services that will search Reuters World Service, Reuters Business Report, and Newsbytes for news on up to 10 topics that you specify. Current clippings are available to download whenever you sign on to GEnie. QuikNews carries a monthly fee of $25.

- GEnie Reference Center (REFCENTER) is a basic reference resource including information on business, technology, and medicine. Each group search costs $2.50, with title reviews at $4.50 (for up to 10 titles) and full-text reviews at $4.50.

- Law Center (LAWCENTER) provides material on a variety of legal topics. Prices vary, depending on the type of search.

- Medical Professional's Center (MEDPRO) contains reference materials on medicine, nursing, psychology, and health care administration including the full text of the *New England Journal of Medicine* and the American Medical Association journals. A group search is priced at $2.50; complete records are $4.50.

- Newsbytes News Network (NEWSBYTES) is a computer industry news service that contains news stories from around the world on computer hardware and software, telecommunications, and computer business trends. No surcharge.

- NewsStand (NEWSSTAND) offers more than 900 full-text newspapers, magazines, and newsletters. Prices vary, depending on the type of search.

- Trademark Center (TRADEMARK) offers a database of more than 1.2 registered trademarks from the U.S., Canada, and the U.K. The database is priced at $2.50 for a group search and $7.50 for individual records.

- Worldwide Patent Center (PATENTS) contains patent records from the U.S. and 30 other countries. A group search costs $2.50; a full patent record is $7.50.

Researching Specific Online Databases

Most of your research needs can probably be met through one of the above on-line services. However, you still might want to have direct access to the information providers that offer the actual databases. In some cases, they will provide data that isn't available anywhere else, particularly if you want to research a highly specialized subject. Following are descriptions of some of the best.

DataStar   An excellent source of science, technology, and European business information. Includes a gateway to Microbial Strain Data Network (biotechnology), Official Airlines Guide, European Railway Guide, and Tradeline (worldwide security pricing and exchange rates). Some sample databases are

- TradStat World Trade Statistics, which covers official government import/export figures for the U.S. and Canada, several countries in South America and the Far East as well as most of Europe, including the newly freed nations of Eastern Europe.

- Medline, which comprises the entire medical field including dentistry, veterinary medicine, and pharmacology with 300,000 new articles each year from 3,500 journals.

- Italian Company Profiles, with financial data on nearly 3,500 Italian companies to carry out market research, target customers, and find potential targets for mergers or acquisitions.

DIALOG   One of the world's best known database providers with comprehensive coverage in many fields. Dialog has news—**new**sletters, newspapers, and newswires—as well as information on patents, medicine, law, technology, company financial reports, and science from both a national and international perspective. Some sample databases are

- Employee Benefits Infosource, which covers all facets of employee benefits planning in the U.S. and Canada.

- Energy Science and Technology, which offers the U.S. Department of Energy databases on energy-related topics.

Asia-Pacific Business Journals, which includes the full text of major Asian and Pacific journals.

 Federal Research in Progress, which covers scientific and engineering research funded by the U.S. government.

 Oceanic Abstracts, which offers abstracts on marine-related topics.

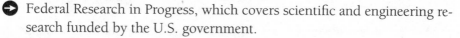 **The Knight-Ridder Dialog home page**

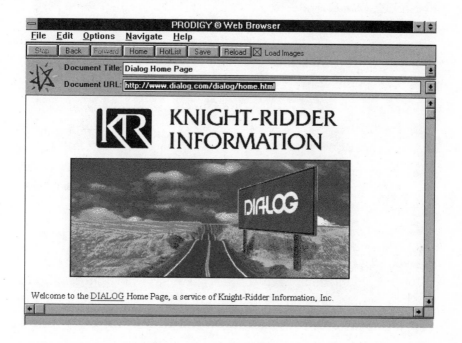

Dow Jones News/Retrieval   Dow Jones focuses on business and financial information with access to thousands of business-related trade journal, magazine, newspaper, and newsletter articles as well as exclusive coverage of the *Wall Street*

Journal and *Barron's*. Dow Jones also provides company/industry profiles, investment quotes, technical analysis, SEC filing extracts and earnings forecasts. Coverage is international. Some examples are

 Mutual Funds Performance Report, which covers the historical performance and background of 1,500 mutual funds.

 SEC Online, which provides the full text of 10Ks, 10Qs, annual reports, and proxy filings for more than 11,000 public companies.

 Tradeline, which offers up to 20 years of historical information on stocks, bonds, indexes, and foreign exchange rates.

Dow Jones also recently introduced the *Personal Journal*, a customized electronic version of *The Wall Street Journal*. By setting up a personal news profile and personal portfolio, you get only the exact information you need.

LEXIS•NEXIS   The LEXIS•NEXIS services focus on legal and business information. LEXIS provides access to 45 specialized libraries covering federal, state, tax, securities, banking, environmental, energy, and international law. NEXIS covers business and news from around the world with more than 2,400 full-text sources.

NewsNet   This is primarily a source of hundreds of industry newsletters but also contains 20 international newswires as well as financial/investment information. Some samples include the following:

 Ice Cream Reporter, which covers and analyzes the ice cream industry.

Law Office Technology Review, which evaluates office technology (particularly computer software) designed for the law office.

Multimedia Publisher, with monthly reports on news, trends, and marketing strategies of multimedia producers.

Questel•Orbit   A database provider specializing in patents, trademarks, European business, chemistry, science, and technology. Since Questel is a

The opening screen of Dow Jones's Personal Journal

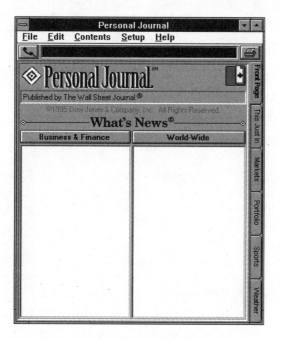

Europe-based company (with a U.S. office in Virginia), their databases are in many languages—French, German, and English are the most common. Some useful English-language databases include

 Cold, with everything you could want to know about the Arctic and Antarctica. Over 156,000 technical documents on snow, ice, navigation, and civil engineering in cold temperatures.

 Derwent's World Patents Index, which covers patents around the world, with millions of records.

 Enviroline, with over 187,000 records on the environment—air, land, and water.

- ➔ Meeting Agenda, which contains announcements of meetings, conferences, and exhibitions around the world, particularly in the fields of science, medicine, and technology.
- ➔ Tropical Agriculture, which covers worldwide literature since 1975 on agriculture in tropical and subtropical regions.
- ➔ Who's Who in Technology, which provides detailed biographies of 37,000 leaders in American technology.

Search Suggestions

The following suggested areas provide the most comprehensive coverage in a specific area and/or the most economical way to access specific information.

If You Want	Try
Basic news	Newsgrid, Executive News Service
Comprehensive research on a variety of topics	DIALOG
Computer industry news	Newsbytes, Computer Database Plus
Financial information	Dow Jones News/Retrieval
General-purpose research	Knowledge Index
International business information	DataStar
Legal information	LEXIS
Medical Information	Medline
Newspapers	Knowledge Index, NewsStand, Dow Jones News/Retrieval
Patent and trademark information	Questel•Orbit
Travel information	OAG

➜ Six Steps to Successful Online Database Searching

1. Determine what you need to know.
2. Find out which database providers offer that information.
3. Compare costs. The same databases offered by different providers can be priced differently.
4. Learn how to use the system. Database providers often provide low-cost or free training to new users or offer free online time to help you get acquainted with their system.
5. Develop a search strategy and put it in writing. Where do you need to go to get the information you need? Are there any shortcuts?
6. Get the information you need and get offline quickly.

Contact Information for the Top Research Services

Company	Phone	World Wide Web Site
CompuServe	800-848-8199	http://www.compuserve.com
Dow Jones News/Retrieval	800-522-3567	N/A
GEnie	800-638-9636	http://www.genie.com
Knight-Ridder Information (DIALOG and DataStar)	800-334-2564	http://www.dialog.com
LEXIS•NEXIS	800-227-4908	http://www.lexis-nexis.com
NewsNet	800-345-1301	N/A
Questel•Orbit	800-955-0906	http://www.questel.orbit.com

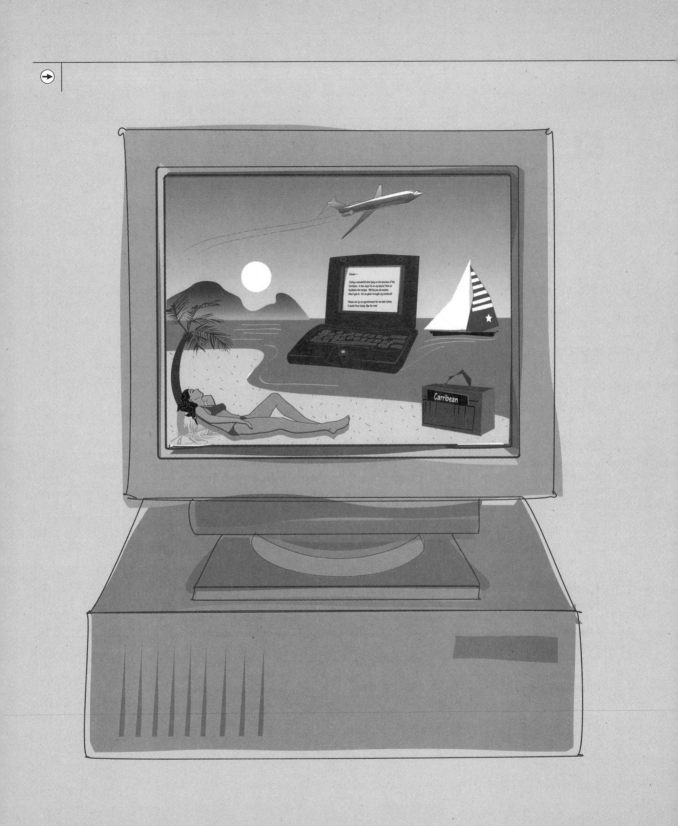

11

Telecommuting Away from Home

Notebook

computers are lighter, more powerful, and less expensive than they have ever been, and that's good news for today's "road warriors" who rely on mobile computing to do their jobs and keep in touch with their offices. But even if bringing your computer with you is much easier than in the past, you still may need to overcome some obstacles to using and connecting your computer to the outside world when you travel.

Mobile Computing in the Air

The basic rule for in-flight computing is not to use your computer during takeoff or landing, or at elevations of less than 10,000 feet. Since policies can vary from airline to airline, it's best to check with your carrier before your trip if you have any questions.

You can also get some work done on the ground while you're waiting for your flight. Many airline clubs for business travelers provide phones with modem connections, fax machines, copiers, printers, and other business services useful to the computer-carrying traveler.

Hotel Amenities for Road Warriors

As more and more hotels realize that today's business travelers require access to current technology, the amenities for mobile computing are increasing. All of the largest business hotel chains in the U.S. provide dataports for modem use as well as access to printers, fax machines, and copiers in all or many of their locations. Some examples include:

➔ Hyatt Hotels offers a special Hyatt Business Plan that provides a room equipped with a fax machine, a workstation with enhanced lighting suitable for a computer user, and two phone lines for $15 extra per night. These computer-friendly rooms are located in a special section of the hotel that provides 24-hour access to business machines such as copiers and printers.

The Marriott chain provides dataports in most hotel rooms as well as access to a 24-hour business center with copiers, fax machines, and printers.

➡ Hilton's BusinessSavers program includes in-room dataports as well as access to business centers that provide fax machines, printers, and copiers.

➡ Sheraton has in-room dataport connections in many of its hotels. Business centers provide access to printers, fax machines, and copiers.

Some independent hotels are also very computer-friendly:

➡ The Nob Hill Lambourne in San Francisco offers an IBM-compatible computer and a fax machine in every guest room as well as a dataport. Their business center is equipped with a printer and copier and is accessible 24 hours a day. Rates vary from $145 to $225 a night depending on the size of the room.

➡ The Tutor in New York City offers dual-line phones with dataports as well as access to copiers, fax machines, and printers during regular business hours in their business center. Rates range from $195 to $265 a night.

➡ Inn at the Market in Seattle provides in-room fax machines and dataports in their suites. Room rates vary from $275 to $300 a night, based on location.

If high-tech amenities are essential to you when you travel, be sure to check with the individual hotel before you register, since you may need to request a specific room to suit your needs. Even with the chain hotels, the facilities vary from location to location.

Mobile Computing Overseas

 International travelers face additional problems—they need to negotiate a maze of varying phone plugs, modems, and telecommunications systems before successfully connecting in a foreign country.

Computer Products Plus has created a special "survival kit" for road warriors venturing overseas. Its Tele-Travel Kit International, retailing for $229.95, includes the Telecoupler II high speed modem coupler, screwdriver, magnifier/flashlight, printer cable, modular line cord, and international power plug and telephone adapters. The coupler is a device that plugs into your computer's modem and attaches to a telephone handset, allowing you to communicate over pay, cellular, or hotel phones that aren't properly equipped for modem communications. Travelers who aren't leaving the U.S., but still have difficulty connecting their notebook computers, may be interested in the domestic version of this product, the Tele-Traveler Kit.

➡ Other Things to Bring

- ➡ Disks—including spare blank disks, a boot disk, and backup disks of important files

- ➡ Local access phone numbers for any online service you use

- ➡ Spare notebook computer battery

- ➡ Printer cable, or portable printer, if you're not sure about the availability of an on-site printer

Resources for the High-Tech Traveler

Company	Number
Computer Products Plus	800-274-4277
Hilton Hotels	800-445-8667
Hyatt Hotels	800-233-1234
Inn at the Market	800-446-4484
Marriott Hotels	800-228-9290

Resources for the High-Tech Traveler (Continued)

Company	Number
Nob Hill Lambourne	800-274-8466
Sheraton Hotels	800-325-3535
The Tutor	800-879-8836

Appendix A:
Resources for Telecommuters

The following resources will help you set up an efficient telecommuting system.

Handbooks and Booklets

Telecommuting: A Handbook to Help You Set Up a Program at Your Company. California Department of Transportation in cooperation with the U.S. Department of Transportation. 415-861-7665.

Telecommuting Guidelines for Telecommuters and Telecommuting Guidelines for Supervisors. Economic Development Partnership. 2150 Webster Street, Room 1000, Oakland, CA 94612. 510-645-0673.

Telecommuting Resource Guide. Pacific Bell. 800-378-1980.

Books

The Complete Work-at-Home Companion, by Herman Holtz. Prima Publishing (1990).

The Joy of Working from Home, by Jeff Berner. Berrett-Koehler Publishers (1994).

The Work-at-Home Sourcebook, by Lynie Arden. Live Oak Publications (1988).

Working from Home, by Paul and Sarah Edwards. Putnam (1994).

Magazines

Home Office Computing, 730 Broadway, New York, NY 10003. 800-866-5821.

Mobile Office, P.O. Box 57267, Boulder, CO 80322-7267. 800-627-5234.

Newsletters

Success Working from Home, Jeff Berner, P.O. Box 244, Dillon Beach, CA 94929.

Telecommuting Review, Telespan Publishing Corporation, 50 West Palm Street, Altadena, CA 91001. 818-797-5482.

The Kern Report: Trends and Issues in Home-Based Business and Telecommuting, P.O. Box 14850, Chicago, IL 60614.

Appendix B:
Vendor Technical Support

As detailed in Chapter 8, there are three main ways to get vendor technical support: by telephone, by fax, and online.

Because of the low prices of many of today's popular applications, most vendors now only provide free telephone support for a limited time, for example, for the first 30 to 90 days. After that, in most cases you must pay for continuing support. The good news, however, is that many companies offer extensive technical support resources both online and via fax that are free to end users. Microsoft's KnowledgeBase and the Lotus Technical Library are just two examples of the type of rich resources available in a searchable format.

Computer vendors have devoted a lot of time and effort to creating numerous technical support options in order to stay competitive in the marketplace. Microsoft, for example, offers free support for 30 to 90 days for many of its products. Afterward, users have the option of paying $2.95 per minute for support or participating in an annual fee-based support plan. They also provide the 35,000-document KnowledgeBase on several online services and offer a fax-on-demand system. Borland offers free Up & Running support to answer installation and configuration questions, and Advisor Lines support at $2.00 per minute for more advanced questions on usability, as well as several fee-based annual support contracts. Borland also provides technical support on several online services as well as via fax.

Before you call a vendor technical support line, attempt to

- Find the answer in the user manual or online help first. Many manuals contain a troubleshooting section that could provide you with an immediate answer.
- Isolate the problem as best as you can. Is the program not working at all? Or does it only not work under certain circumstances? Are you sure it's a problem with the software and not with the hardware or system itself? A good way to check this is to see if other application programs still work as expected.

➡ Have your serial number or user ID ready to give to the support representative. You must be a registered user to get technical support and provide proof of this before your questions can be answered.

Vendor Support Quick Reference

The following table details how to get technical support from the vendors of today's best-selling products.

Vendor	Telephone	Fax	Online
Microsoft	206-635-7056	800-936-4100	America Online. Keyword: Microsoft BBS. 206-936-6735 CompuServe. GO MICROSOFT GEnie. MICROSOFT Internet WWW. http://www.microsoft.com
Lotus	508-988-2500	800-346-3508	Internet: http://www.lotus.com
Apple	800-SOS-APPL		eWorld. Apple Customer Center
Borland	800-523-7070	800-822-4269	BIX. JOIN BORLAND BBS. 408-431-5096 CompuServe. GO BORLAND GEnie. BORLAND Internet WWW. http://www.borland.com
WordPerfect	800-861-2729	800-228-9960	BBS. 801-225-4414 CompuServe. GO WPFILES or GO WPUSERS GEnie. WP Internet WWW. http://www.wordperfect.com

Because of the variety of telephone support options, and the fact that many vendors have a different number for each product, one basic number is provided to get you connected with the company. To get technical support information on other products you own, refer to the user manual or online help for contact information.

Appendix C:
How to Use the CD-ROM

The CD-ROM accompanying this book can make working from a home or mobile office even easier! Included are several complete shareware programs, your online connection to CompuServe via WinCIM, information on other Ziff-Davis Press books, a multimedia demo of the book *How Computers Work*, and more. Here's what you need to use the CD-ROM:

- → IBM-compatible PC
- → 386DX-33 (486DX-33 or faster recommended)
- → 4MB RAM (minimum)
- → 4MB available on the hard drive
- → VGA color display (8-bit 256 color display highly recommended)
- → Microsoft mouse or 100 percent compatible
- → MS-DOS 3.0 or higher
- → Microsoft Windows 3.1 or higher
- → CD-ROM drive (double-speed recommended)
- → Sound card and associated drivers installed (for product demos)

Installing the CD-ROM

To install the YOUR HOME OFFICE CD-ROM directly onto your computer, select Run from the File menu in the Windows Program Manager. On the command line, type **D:\INSTALL.EXE** (if your CD-ROM isn't drive D, substitute the appropriate drive letter here) and press OK. This will create a Ziff-Davis Press program group. Don't forget to read the README file that appears in the program group where you installed the CD-ROM. To run the CD-ROM directly without installing it on the desktop, select Run from the File menu and enter **D:\RUN_ME.EXE** on the command line. If you're using Windows 95, select the Start button and choose Run from the menu.

When you start the CD-ROM, you will see four sections listed on the screen:

- Software Samples
- Shareware
- Online Service
- More from Ziff-Davis Press

For more information on any of these topics, select its corresponding icon. To move around the CD-ROM, use the Home, Previous, Next, and Quit icons at the bottom of each screen. To deactivate the background music and transitions, press F10 and remove the checkmarks from the appropriate boxes.

Accessing the Software Samples

To access the two software samples, Personal Journal and DiskNet, you must first download the programs to your computer. Here's what you'll find and how to run it.

Personal Journal   Personal Journal is an interactive, customizable version of The Wall Street Journal. The CD-ROM includes complete software to connect to the service, as well as a two-week trial membership. Personal Journal allows you to scan the headlines, view news about weather, sports, and the market, as well as to track the latest news and quotes on your favorite stocks and mutual funds. To obtain a password to use this program, you must first call Dow Jones Customer Service at 800-291-9382, ext. 831.

To install Personal Journal click on its icon to open the Installation dialog box. The program will install to C:\PJ by default. If you want to install it to another directory or drive, select the Set Location button. Enter the new location (D:\PJ, for example) and click on OK to return to the previous dialog box. Once the program has been installed on your computer, you can access it by clicking on the Personal Journal icon in the Personal Journal program group. To set up Personal Journal to your preferences, follow the on-screen Setup Assistant.

When prompted for a password, enter the password you received when you called Dow Jones Customer Service.

DiskNet   DiskNet is a virus protection program. To install the trial software, click on the DiskNet virus protection icon, select your desired directory, and click OK. By default, the files are placed in C:\DISKNET. Run the file DNINSTAL.EXE to install DiskNet.

Accessing the Shareware

To install any of the following four shareware programs on your computer, click on the program's icon, enter the destination directory (the default directories are listed below), and click OK.

Frequent Flyer Manager 5.0 helps you track and manage your frequent flyer miles. To install this program, run INSTALLD.EXE in the C:\FFLYER directory. The installation program will create a new directory called C:\FFM. Run FFM.EXE from this new directory to use the program. Remember that you can run any program in Windows 3.1 by selecting File and Run from the menu. In Windows 95, you can run a program by selecting the Start button and choosing Run from the menu.

Understanding the Internet is a Windows help file that provides lots of useful information about the Internet. To view this file, run UNDER.HLP in the C:\UNDR_INT directory.

PKZip 2.04 is a file compression utility that allows you to archive and unarchive compressed files. To compress files, run PKZIP.EXE in the C:\PKZIP204 directory; to decompress files run PKUNZIP.EXE. MANUAL.DOC offers complete details on how to use this useful program.

~☐~

Business Letters includes more than 600 sample business letter templates that cover a wide variety of topics. These are found in C:\BUSLTR and are in a text format readable by most word processors.

Accessing the Online Service

ZiffNet is available via the CompuServe online information service. This book includes a free one-month membership to both ZiffNet and CompuServe, as well as a free Windows program called WinCIM, which is designed to access the service. To download WinCIM, click on the Online Service icon from the main screen of the CD-ROM. Click on the I Agree/Install icon, select your desired directory, and click OK to download the software to your computer. To set up the program run WINCIM.EXE in the C:\CSERVE directory.

Accessing More from Ziff-Davis Press

This section contains more information about Ziff-Davis Press, a book catalog and order form, as well as a multimedia demo of *How Computers Work*. To access, click on the More from Ziff-Davis Press icon on the CD-ROM's main screen.

Index

Allegro software
  Business 500, 94
  Business Library, 94–95
  Learn to Do Word
    Processing, 86
  New Media, 85
America Online,
    connecting to,
    65–66
America Online
    information
  about antivirus
    programs, 77
  about CD-ROM drives
    and titles, 29
  about communications
    software, 46
  about fax/modems, 22
  about printers, 25
  about tape backup
    systems, 33
AntiVirus for Macintosh
    4.0 (Symantec), 76
Apple Technical
    Information Library,
    89

backup strategies, 30–31
  determining your
    needs, 30–33
  suggested systems,
    31–32
battery life of notebooks,
    14
books for telecommuters,
    122
Bookshelf (Microsoft), 99
Business Database Plus,
    105
Business 500 (Allegro), 94
Business Library
    (Allegro), 94–95
business shareware,
    finding, 100
buying a computer
    system, 9–16

Carbon Copy 2.5
    (Microcom), 53
CD-R (recordable CD), 30
CD-ROM drives, 27–29
Close-Up 6.0 (Norton-
    Lambert), 53–54
college classes, 84

communications port
    settings, 37–38
communications software,
    35, 38–44
  getting information
    about, 46–47
  selecting, 36–37
  vendor information,
    45–46
Compton's Interactive
    Encyclopedia 3.0,
    95–96
CompuServe
  Basic service, 63
  connecting to, 62–65
  online research,
    104–107
  Premium service,
    63–64
  pricing plans, 64–65
  reference menu, 106
  technical support
    from, 89–90
CompuServe information
  about antivirus
    programs, 77
  about CD-ROM drives
    and titles, 29
  about communications
    software, 46
  about fax/modems, 22

Symantec Norton pcANYWHERE 2.0 (Symantec), 55
systems
  choosing, 9–16
  manufacturers, 15
  tips for purchasing, 15–16
  where to purchase, 14–15
system utility software, 87–88

tape backup systems, 33
technical support
  from a distance, 83–91
  resources, 91
  from vendors, 88–90, 124–126
telecommuters and telecommuting
  advantages of, 4–5
  data security risks of, 78
  disadvantages of, 4–5
  isolation of, 5
  mobile, 117–121
  online forums for, 71
  resources for, 122–123
  and staying on the fast track, 5–6

and time management, 6
tips for, 6–7
types of, 3–4
Telecommuting Resource Guide, 4
telephone support from vendors, 88
Teneron LegalPoint 1.0, 99
Timbuktu Pro for Macintosh (Farallon), 52–53
time management, 6
Trademark Center, 109
Trademarkscan, 107
Traveling Software's Laplink for Windows, 55–56
Triton CoSession for Windows 2.0, 55

user groups, learning from, 87
utility software, using, 87–88

vendor technical support, 88–90, 124–126
Viagrafix, 85

video training, 84–85
viruses, protecting data from, 74–77

Windows 95, faxing with, 39
WinFax PRO 4.0, 41
Worldwide Patent Center, 109
World Wide Web (WWW), 70

ZiffNet Support On Site, 89

USE YOUR COMPUTER TO
SAVE MONEY
SAVE TIME
IN EVERY ASPECT OF YOUR LIFE

YOUR MONEY
1-56276-301-6
$24.95

SMART TRAVEL
1-56276-307-5
$24.95

YOUR CHILD'S EDUCATION
1-56276-314-8 $24.95

Aimed at the millions of people who are taking the computer beyond the workplace and into their homes, each Total Planning book presents a comprehensive strategy that any computer user can follow to organize and improve their life.

Every book comes with $15 of free online time, a CD-ROM packed with software, shareware, worksheets and demos of some of the best CD-ROM software around.

FREE: $15 of Online Time

YOUR ROOTS
1-56276-326-1 $24.95

HOME IMPROVEMENT
1-56276-334-2 $24.95

YOUR HOME OFFICE
1-56276-327-X $24.95

YOUR HEALTH
1-56276-302-4 $24.95

ZIFF-DAVIS ZD PRESS

©1995 Ziff-Davis Press

Available at all fine bookstores or call 1-800-688-0448, ext. 352.

Ride the Fast Lane on the Information Highway

Driving lessons for online newcomers. The latest waves for expert net surfers.

In these just-released books from Ziff-Davis Press, noted authors share their passion for the online world. Join them on a thrilling ride down the information highway from the comfort of your home or office.

THE INTERNET VIA MOSAIC AND WORLD-WIDE WEB

$24.95 ISBN: 1-56276-259-1

PC Magazine UK Labs Manager Steve Browne focuses on Mosaic, the most popular Web browser. Browne concisely explains how to gain access to the Web and how to take advantage of the Web's hyper-linked environment through Mosaic. Included are valuable discussions on the ways business can take advantage of the Web.

HOW TO USE THE INTERNET

$17.95 ISBN: 1-56276-222-2

Colorfully illustrated how-to guide; the easiest way for beginning Internet users to have fun and get productive fast.

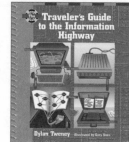

THE TRAVELER'S GUIDE TO THE INFORMATION HIGHWAY

$24.95 ISBN: 1-56276-206-0

The ultimate atlas to online resources including CompuServe, America Online, the Internet, and more.

THE INTERNET BY E-MAIL

$19.95 ISBN: 1-56276-240-0

Fun and informative Internet services available at no extra charge from the e-mail system you already know.

BUILDING THE INFORMATION HIGHWAY

$24.95 ISBN: 1-56276-126-9

Our present and future information structure, delightfully illustrated and clearly explained for anyone who's curious.

HOW THE INTERNET WORKS

$24.95 ISBN: 1-56276-192-7

Best-selling, full-color presentation of the technological marvel that links people and communities throughout the world.

The Quick and Easy Way to Learn.

Teaches Windows 3.1
The Quick and Easy Way to Learn
ISBN: 1-56276-051-3
Price: $22.95

Teaches WordPerfect 6.0
The Quick and Easy Way to Learn
ISBN: 1-56276-105-6
Price: $22.95

Teaches Word 6.0 for Windows
The Quick and Easy Way to Learn
ISBN: 1-56276-139-0
Price: $22.95

We know that PC Learning Labs books are the fastest and easiest way to learn because years have been spent perfecting them. Beginners will find practice sessions that are easy to follow and reference information that is easy to find. Even the most computer-shy readers can gain confidence faster than they ever thought possible.

The time we spent designing this series translates into time saved for you. You can feel confident that the information is accurate and presented in a way that allows you to learn quickly and effectively.

Teaches Microsoft Access 2.0
The Quick and Easy Way to Learn
ISBN: 1-56276-225-7
Price: $22.95

Teaches FoxPro 2.5 for Windows
The Quick and Easy Way to Learn
ISBN: 1-56276-176-5
Price: $22.95

Teaches CorelDRAW! 4.0
The Quick and Easy Way to Learn
ISBN: 1-56276-188-9
Price: $22.95

Teaches Microsoft Office
The Quick and Easy Way to Learn
ISBN: 1-56276-272-9
Price: $22.95

Teaches WordPerfect 6.0 for Windows
The Quick and Easy Way to Learn
ISBN: 1-56276-020-3
Price: $22.95

Teaches Ami Pro 3.0
The Quick and Easy Way to Learn
ISBN: 1-56276-134-X
Price: $22.95

Teaches Microsoft Project 4.0 for Windows
The Quick and Easy Way to Learn
ISBN: 1-56276-226-5
Price: $22.95

Teaches Excel 5.0 for Windows
The Quick and Easy Way to Learn
ISBN: 1-56276-141-2
Price: $22.95

Teaches 1-2-3 4.0 for Windows
The Quick and Easy Way to Learn
ISBN: 1-56276-199-4
Price: $22.95

Teaches DOS 6.2
The Quick and Easy Way to Learn
ISBN: 1-56276-100-5
Price: $22.95

Teaches PowerPoint 4.0 for Windows
The Quick and Easy Way to Learn
ISBN: 1-56276-229-X
Price: $22.95

Teaches NetWare 3.12
The Quick and Easy Way to Learn
ISBN: 1-56276-253-2
Price: $22.95

Also available: Titles featuring new versions of FoxPro, 1-2-3, Ami Pro, and new applications, pending software release. Call 1-800-688-0448 for title update information.

ZIFF-DAVIS ZD PRESS

Available at all fine bookstores, or by calling 1-800-688-0448, ext. 276. For Corporate/ Government programs, call (800) 488-8741 ext. 297. For Education programs, call (800) 786-6541.

Ziff-Davis Press Survey of Readers

Please help us in our effort to produce the best books on personal computing.
For your assistance, we would be pleased to send you a FREE catalog
featuring the complete line of Ziff-Davis Press books.

1. How did you first learn about this book?

Recommended by a friend . . . . ☐ -1 (5)

Recommended by store personnel . . . . ☐ -2

Saw in Ziff-Davis Press catalog . . . . ☐ -3

Received advertisement in the mail . . . . ☐ -4

Saw the book on bookshelf at store . . . . ☐ -5

Read book review in: _____ ☐ -6

Saw an advertisement in: _____ ☐ -7

Other (Please specify): _____ ☐ -8

2. Which THREE of the following factors most influenced your decision to purchase this book? (Please check up to THREE.)

Front or back cover information on book . . . ☐ -1 (6)

Logo of magazine affiliated with book . . . . . . ☐ -2

Special approach to the content . . . . ☐ -3

Completeness of content . . . . ☐ -4

Author's reputation. . . . . ☐ -5

Publisher's reputation . . . . ☐ -6

Book cover design or layout . . . . ☐ -7

Index or table of contents of book . . . . ☐ -8

Price of book . . . . ☐ -9

Special effects, graphics, illustrations . . . . ☐ -0

Other (Please specify): _____ ☐ -x

3. How many computer books have you purchased in the last six months? _____ (7-10)

4. On a scale of 1 to 5, where 5 is excellent, 4 is above average, 3 is average, 2 is below average, and 1 is poor, please rate each of the following aspects of this book below. (Please circle your answer.)

Depth/completeness of coverage	5 4 3 2 1	(11)
Organization of material	5 4 3 2 1	(12)
Ease of finding topic	5 4 3 2 1	(13)
Special features/time saving tips	5 4 3 2 1	(14)
Appropriate level of writing	5 4 3 2 1	(15)
Usefulness of table of contents	5 4 3 2 1	(16)
Usefulness of index	5 4 3 2 1	(17)
Usefulness of accompanying disk	5 4 3 2 1	(18)
Usefulness of illustrations/graphics	5 4 3 2 1	(19)
Cover design and attractiveness	5 4 3 2 1	(20)
Overall design and layout of book	5 4 3 2 1	(21)
Overall satisfaction with book	5 4 3 2 1	(22)

5. Which of the following computer publications do you read regularly; that is, 3 out of 4 issues?

Byte . . . . ☐ -1 (23)

Computer Shopper . . . . ☐ -2

Home Office Computing . . . . ☐ -3

Dr. Dobb's Journal . . . . ☐ -4

LAN Magazine . . . . ☐ -5

MacWEEK . . . . ☐ -6

MacUser . . . . ☐ -7

PC Computing . . . . ☐ -8

PC Magazine . . . . ☐ -9

PC WEEK . . . . ☐ -0

Windows Sources . . . . ☐ -x

Other (Please specify): _____ ☐ -y

Please turn page.

6. What is your level of experience with personal computers? With the subject of this book?

	With PCs	With subject of book
Beginner........	☐ -1 (24)	☐ -1 (25)
Intermediate....	☐ -2	☐ -2
Advanced........	☐ -3	☐ -3

7. Which of the following best describes your job title?

Officer (CEO/President/VP/owner)........ ☐ -1 (26)
Director/head........................... ☐ -2
Manager/supervisor..................... ☐ -3
Administration/staff.................... ☐ -4
Teacher/educator/trainer............... ☐ -5
Lawyer/doctor/medical professional....... ☐ -6
Engineer/technician.................... ☐ -7
Consultant............................ ☐ -8
Not employed/student/retired........... ☐ -9
Other (Please specify): _____ ☐ -0

8. What is your age?

Under 20............................. ☐ -1 (27)
21-29................................ ☐ -2
30-39................................ ☐ -3
40-49................................ ☐ -4
50-59................................ ☐ -5
60 or over........................... ☐ -6

9. Are you:

Male................................. ☐ -1 (28)
Female............................... ☐ -2

Thank you for your assistance with this important information! Please write your address below to receive our free catalog.

Name: _____

Address: _____

City/State/Zip: _____

Fold here to mail.

327X-16-20

‖‖‖‖

BUSINESS REPLY MAIL

FIRST CLASS MAIL   PERMIT NO. 1612   OAKLAND, CA

POSTAGE WILL BE PAID BY ADDRESSEE

Ziff-Davis Press
ZIFF-DAVIS
ZD
PRESS
5903 Christie Avenue
Emeryville, CA 94608-1925
Attn: Marketing

‖‖|‖‖‖|‖‖‖‖|‖|‖‖‖|‖‖‖|‖|‖‖‖|‖‖|‖‖|‖‖|‖‖‖|